ACCOUNTING SERVICES, THE INTERNATIONAL ECONOMY, AND THIRD WORLD DEVELOPMENT

ACCOUNTING SERVICES, THE INTERNATIONAL ECONOMY, AND THIRD WORLD DEVELOPMENT

David L. McKee
and Don E. Garner

PRAEGER

Westport, Connecticut
London

Library of Congress Cataloging-in-Publication Data

McKee, David L.
   Accounting services, the international economy, and Third World
development / David L. McKee and Don E. Garner.
     p.   cm.
   Includes bibliographical references.
   ISBN 0-275-94115-9 (alk. paper)
   1. Accounting firms. 2. International business enterprises—
Accounting. 3. Developing countries—Economic conditions.
I. Garner, Don E. II. Title.
HF5627.M35 1992
338.7'6165796—dc20   92-16548

British Library Cataloguing in Publication Data is available.

Library of Congress Catalog Card Number: 92-16548
ISBN: 0-275-94115-9

First published in 1992

Praeger Publishers, 88 Post Road West, Westport, CT 06881
An imprint of Greenwood Publishing Group, Inc.

Printed in the United States of America

The paper used in this book complies with the
Permanent Paper Standard issued by the National
Information Standards Organization (Z39.48–1984).

10   9   8   7   6   5   4   3   2   1

Contents

Acknowledgments

In preparing this book the intention has been to provide insights into the impacts that the major accounting firms are having upon the global economy and, more specifically, upon the development potential of Third World nations.

The research underlying the project was funded in part by a research, scholarship, and creative activity grant awarded by California State University, Stanislaus.

From the inception of the project, the authors have benefitted from the input or support of various individuals. Among those who should be thanked are Hans Husman, who served effectively as a research assistant, and Arthur S. Costa, whose assistance went well beyond his professional duties in the library of California State University, Stanislaus.

Others who contributed to the success of the project were Robert T. Sullens, professor emeritus, John Carroll University, and James D. Cigler, international tax partner, Price Waterhouse. The Sacramento office of KPMG Peat Marwick International provided considerable valuable information.

A special thanks is deserved by Linda Poje, who was indispensable in the editing and typing of the manuscript and in seeing it through its various drafts.

None of those who have helped should share the blame for any shortcomings that may be perceived in the final project.

Introduction

Not too long ago an editorial in *The Economist* proclaimed that "auditors are capitalism's handmaidens" (July 15, 1989, 18) and went on to suggest that "unless they [the auditors] provide and are seen to provide accurate, honest and impartial information on companies, the whole structure of competitive market economies will be threatened." Even stripped of its drama, that appraisal of the role of auditing in market-driven economies appears to be accurate. To continue to function effectively, such economies must have up-to-date, dependable financial records of where they have been. Only with such information can they attempt effective assessments of where they may be going and, with those assessments in hand, institute both private and public policies designed to assist them on their journeys.

In advanced nations the public accounting firms appear to be at center stage with respect to supplying auditing services. By exercising that supply function, they have joined various other business and financial service firms that have become the facilitators which appear to lubricate the operations of advanced business-oriented economies. In many cases accounting firms reach beyond their main auditing functions to provide tax counseling and various other managerial advisory services. In these latter endeavors they may also overlap (compete with) services provided by other types of practitioners. By doing so it appears as though they are strengthening their own positions while, at the same time, deepening their facilitative role in the economies in question.

The fact that services in general have come to dominate the labor force statistics of advanced nations will not be reviewed in the current investigation. The idea of service ascendancy is no longer controversial (Stanback et al., 1981; McKee and Bennett 1987; Cohen and Zysman, 1988; McKee, 1987). In the interests of conserving space, little attention will be devoted to general discussion of the role of various service subgroups as facilitators (see McKee, 1988).

The intent here is to go beyond the types of general positioning and to consider the role of accounting and related services in the processes of expansion and change under capitalism. In the present context it will be necessary to become more general in order to reach an understanding of the specifics in question, since capitalism is international in scope. Today the public accounting firms are carrying out their operations in the international economy. In doing so, they themselves have become multinational firms. The impact of the business that they transact is being felt in the international economy as well as in those of their home nations, not to mention the economies that host their clients or their own branch offices, subsidiaries, and cooperating domestic firms.

Although the impact of the large, multinational accounting firms appears to be becoming worldwide, the present investigation is most interested in the effect that these firms are having on the economies of emerging nations. More specifically, it attempts to address the impact that the firms in question appear to be having upon developmental processes in the Third World.

The parameters of the project are established in the first section of the book where the institutional accounting framework is reviewed. In that section the rise of international accounting firms is reviewed. In that context the international expansion of the service offerings of the firms is shown as a logical consequence of the emergence of multinational corporations. Indeed the expansion of the accounting firms is seen as an effort to service corporate clients, thus establishing from the outset their role as facilitators in the world economy and, of course, in the domestic economies of the nations who have become their hosts.

Following that, the discussion shifts to the causes and effects of the major international differences in accounting standards that have emerged. Although such variations appear to reflect the perceived needs of individual jurisdictions, the implications of their existence for efficiency in the international economy are significant. The groundwork for understanding the problems related to this is established in this chapter. The final chapter of the institutional section deals with the impacts of accounting procedures that are employed within multinational corporations upon the operations of those firms and the jurisdictions that host their components.

In the second section of the book, the emphasis shifts from the accounting framework per se to the economic impact that the accounting firms are having in the world economy as well as in host nations. The section begins with a general discussion of international business services from a developmental standpoint. Here their role as facilitators is emphasized especially as it pertains to Third World settings. Following that, the specific impacts of accounting services in developmental processes are reviewed. With the treatment of such impacts completed, the discussion expands to consider the importance of the ever-growing selection of consulting services that are being offered by the accounting firms. Although such offerings are not always looked upon with favor by those more concerned with traditional accounting services, it was felt that they should be included because of the very real impacts that they can have on developmental processes. The section concludes with a treatment of technology as it enhances the potential impact of the accounting firms.

The final section of the monograph is devoted to pulling together the diverse subsets of the project to insure that the overall developmental implications of what the accounting firms are about are not obscured by the detailing of the issues involved. Here the work of the earlier sections of the book is summarized and an attempt is made to suggest the policy implications of what the firms are doing for Third World jurisdictions concerned with economic expansion.

I

THE INSTITUTIONAL ACCOUNTING FRAMEWORK

1

The Rise of International Accounting Firms

Since earliest times some method has been needed to record and to account for transactions among people and among organizations for purposes of decision making. The world and human transactions have been ever changing over the millennia and, of course, are changing to this day. Accountants adapt their methods and practices reflecting changing human conditions, changing transactions, and changing needs of decision makers. In adapting, advances in accounting services appear to contribute to furthering economic activity and development in the world. Without improved accounting services over time, economic growth might not be possible.

In his *Origin and Evolution of Double Entry Bookkeeping*, Edward Peragallo (1938, 1) comments, "It should be borne in mind that systems of bookkeeping came into being because of the necessity of recording transactions arising out of commerce, industry and government. Bookkeeping is, therefore, dependent on these transactions for its existence and any changes it undergoes are probably best explained in the light of the changes that occur in business methods."

The history of accounting seems to bear out Peragallo's contentions. Many authors describe how accounting services have changed in response to the needs of decision makers as human activities have changed and expanded over the years (Yamey, 1982; Littleton, 1933; Chatfield, 1968; Carey, 1969; Edwards, 1960). Beginning with simple recording methods, accounting has developed and expanded over the centuries to encompass worldwide sets of accounts. The providers of accounting services have likewise changed from the scribes of ancient civilizations to twentieth-century, world-spanning accountants.

Early accounting development was slow, reflecting the small scale and slow pace of early economic activity. The long and slow pace of development is indicated by the fact that double-entry methods of bookkeeping did not come into use until the fourteenth century. Much as happens today, record-keeping methods in earlier times appear to have developed in response to information needs of decision makers in social organizations, governments, and the church.

Early accounting methods and practices were rudimentary. The first reported evidence of record keeping of an accounting nature dates from 4500 B.C. in the Mesopotamian Valley where scribes used clay tablets for record keeping (Keister, 1965). Samuels and Piper (1985, 15–16) observe in their review of historical accounting literature that Egyptian Pharaohs circa 3000 B.C. had a form of internal financial control operating within their treasury. From its first emergence circa 2800 B.C. in Crete, European civilization made use of elementary accounting knowledge "with most of the records being concerned with tax assessment and with inventory records" (Samuels and Piper, 1985, 15–16). The apparent routes of ancient accounting ideas are outlined by these authors with excellent bibliographical references to the historical literature.

A relatively complete description of ancient accounting methods providing information for decision making is reported by Costouros (1979). During the fifth and fourth centuries B.C. the need to manage the Greek state of Athens gave rise to the development and use of a system that included accounting methods. The government of Athens, which controlled nearly all economic resources, caused the development of accounting methods to plan, control, and evaluate Athenian activities.

Ancient civilizations, it is reported, were based in agriculture with small, largely self-sufficient populations. The populace consisted primarily of slaves, serfs, and poor artisans with a few wealthy individuals. Demand for traded goods was limited. Trade that took place was on a barter basis. Supply of goods was small and means of transportation, poor. Record-keeping needs were limited to listings of property available and, perhaps, a recording of receipts and disbursements.

A number of antecedents were necessary before complete accounting systems were possible and needed. These antecedents were discussed by Littleton as the ability to write, together with an efficient and effective medium for writing; the knowledge of arithmetic; the use of money as a medium of exchange; the rights of private property with an accumulation of private capital; and the development of business organizational relationships whereby credit could be given and received and where ownership of assets could be shared by multiple owners (1933, 13).

A number, if not all, of these antecedents were in place at various times in ancient history, yet double-entry bookkeeping was not developed. Littleton suggests that what was lacking was the concept of productive capital and the conditions necessary for productive use of capital on a scale that could be profitable. An accumulation of capital was needed that could, in turn, be used for further production. Littleton observes that there was wealth in the ancient worlds but "the idea of productive capital was not yet present; in that era of an agricultural stage of development there was no occasion to consider capital as a factor in production." The agricultural stages of ancient civilization were to be in Littleton's words, "followed long afterward by an era of handicraft and one of commerce and still later by an industrial era. These later stages were better suited to the development of bookkeeping" (1933, 15).

During the fourteenth century, factors were in place and conditions appear to have been right for development of capital and, hence, double-entry bookkeeping. Complete systems of accounting were needed by growing mercantile organizations that arose in the commercial centers of northern Italy as a by-product of the Crusades. Complete, self-balancing systems of record keeping suitable for the needs of commerce are thought to date from fourteenth-century Italy. As Littleton has described (1933, 17), there "were two elements which were to stimulate a commerce the like of which the world had never seen." One was "a hardy, growing population in northern Europe, developing a taste for distant products and willing to work to get them." The other was "a source of abundant supply now made accessible in the Near East — an area which constituted a connecting link with far eastern countries."

The weight of evidence does suggest that double-entry accounting emerged during these years prior to Luca Paciolo's writing of *Summa de Arithmetica, Geometrica, Proportione et Proportionalita* in 1494. Some claim, however, that double-entry bookkeeping began in India as early as 8000 to 7000 B.C. (Samuels and Piper, 1985, 14–15). It seems plausible that conditions may have been right for the invention of double-entry accounting methods in many places and at many times in human history.

However shrouded the date of first use, the invention was not a trivial matter. Development of double-entry bookkeeping has been cited as the source of the concept of capital. In discussing the development of capital accounting, Sidney Pollard (1963, 113–34) cites the theories of Werner Sombart. Sombart saw the role of accounting at the center of capitalist theory. Double-entry bookkeeping was essential to the development of capitalism, providing systematic quantification from the viewpoint of capitalist theory. It allowed the separation of the owner from capital and thus created an independent entity that could be viewed as a device to maximize income or capital of the owner. Only through double-entry bookkeeping comes the idea of capital: "before double-entry bookkeeping the category of 'capital' did not exist, and it would not exist now but for it" Sombart wrote (Pollard, 1963, 14).

Pollard traces the development of accounting from early times to the industrial revolution. He saw capitalist development as having had two main stages, "the early transformation from money-lending into commercial capitalism, beginning in Italy in the thirteenth and fourteenth centuries, and the development from commercial into industrial capitalism, beginning in Britain in the eighteenth" (1963, 114). In the earlier period, double entry as a rational basis of accounting was developed. In the latter, the need for fixed capital "led economists to evolve the modern concept of capital" (115).

Whether it is the source of the concept of capital or not, the idea of double-entry bookkeeping seems today a natural enough development. Assets in a business entity need to be viewed as jointly owned by creditors and owners. A method is needed to simultaneously account for comingled assets and for separate rights of creditors and owners. The double-entry method performs these functions and is a complete, self-balancing system, which records on a transaction-by-transaction basis. The concept of owner's capital is clearly presented. The power and logic of this simple yet effective method is demonstrated by the fact that it remains today the fundamental model underlying the world's accounting systems, however sophisticated and diverse they may have become.

Once developed, double-entry methods of bookkeeping slowly spread across Europe from Italy in the sixteenth and seventeenth centuries to Spain, Portugal, Germany, the Netherlands, and France as commercial centers developed across Europe and hence to Britain. Development was slow, reflecting the needs of commerce. Many important concepts in accounting were developed over these centuries. Among them, record keeping began to be made for the entity separate and apart from the owners' personal assets. The entity was viewed as continuing in existence with its history being divided into periods of time and including periodic accounting reports complete with accruals and deferrals. Periodic profit was calculated, thereby making distinctions between contributed and earned capital.

Developments were not, of course, uniform from country to country. Methods and practices appear to have been developed and put into use in response to decision makers' needs for activities at hand. Innovations made in one area or in one enterprise were not necessarily adopted by all others. Double entry for example, although certainly widely known by the end of the seventeenth century, was not widely used by British merchants until the nineteenth century (Yamey, 1982, 25).

As economic activities increased in the eighteenth-century Industrial Revolution, the pace of accounting development quickened. Mass production and advances in technology made possible and necessary a quantum increase in the scale of business. Much larger accumulations of fixed assets used over long periods of time required methods that would better account for depreciation. The problems of overhead costs gave rise to cost accounting techniques. Inventory on a much vaster scale had to be accounted for.

Ownership forms evolved from proprietorships and partnerships to limited liability and stock companies. The scale of investment in long-lived assets made clear that accounting records and reports must distinguish between ownership and liabilities and between earned and contributed capital. Government became larger and more complex, requiring new systems of accounting for taxation and for governmental operations.

The rise in the use of accounts was naturally enough accompanied by a rise in the auditing of accounts. The origins of auditing date nearly as far back as the origins of accounting. Edward Boyd, who traced examples of auditing from the time of ancient Egypt, observed, "whenever the advance of civilization brought about the necessity of one man being entrusted to some extent with the property of another the advisability of some kind of check upon the fidelity of the former would become apparent" (Brown, 1905, 74).

The beginnings of British auditing, it appears, may be viewed as dating from the late thirteenth century. Rudimentary audits, suited to the economic activities of the times, were conducted on behalf of lords of manors, citizens of cities such as London and Dublin, and members of guilds. The fiscal officers of London and other towns in 1298, for example, were "audited by a committee consisting of the mayor, aldermen, sheriffs and certain other[s]" (Littleton, 1933, 260). These early audits were to verify the accountability of individuals charged with fiscal responsibilities of manors, towns, and guilds.

The character of auditing remained relatively unchanged during the fourteenth, fifteenth, and sixteenth centuries. Few people could read or write. Few were capable of arithmetic functions using the Roman numerals of the day. To determine whether a fair and honest administration had been accomplished, it was necessary for the facts to be read out to those people who would have the knowledge to recognize errors, omissions, or frauds. Such oral readings of accounts were common practice in large manors, in cities, and in guilds. The designation of the word audit apparently came from these auditory reporting methods.

Littleton (1933, 263) describes auditing in this period of history as being of two types. "In the first, the audit consisted of a more or less public hearing of the results of the fiscal activities of governmental officers by delegated representatives of the citizens." He saw the second type as "a careful scrutiny by a trusted officer of the manor of the 'charge and discharge' accounts of those household officers who had fiscal responsibilities."

In the first type, reading out of details of receipts served the purpose that recorded receipts could be tested against common knowledge or specific knowledge of those hearing the accounts read. The reading of details of payments, it would seem, served the same purpose. The public readings would serve to reduce fraud and misuse of assets. Naturally, the proofing of the arithmetic of receipt and payment accounts was important (Littleton, 1933, 264).

In charge and discharge kinds of audits, the auditor who was an officer of the manor, it seems, verified receipts to such records as lists of land or tenants. Payments were verified to documents such as expenditure warrants. The auditor prepared a statement that combined and verified accounts of other officers of the manor in charge and discharge format.

The success of the manor in improving agricultural output gave economic viability to towns as centers of economic activity where inventions, innovations, and independent ownership of factories led to the end of feudalism and to the greatly increased economic activities of the Industrial Revolution. The highly centralized operations of manors and guilds gave way to towns in which independent manufacturers employed labor for wages. "In place of community isolation, a sea-borne trade, following hard upon explorations which opened new lands, had brought unparalleled expansion of contact with new markets and new sources of supply" (Littleton, 1933, 264). New methods of business, finance, and insurance were developed. The needs of decision makers in this new, expanded, economic environment called for keeping accounts for greatly increased amounts of long-term fixed assets, for periodic profits or losses, for increased credit transactions, and for continuing investments of ever-greater size. Earlier audits designed for stewardship accountability and carried out in auditory fashion began to give way to examination and testing of written records and documents. The rise of the modern auditor had begun. But it would be a slow process.

During the seventeenth and eighteenth centuries as European nations spread their power in colonial spheres of dominion and influence, they took their accounting methods with them. The rise of the British Empire providing raw materials for the Industrial Revolution in England from far-flung colonies spread British accounting practices over major parts of the globe. British accountants first visited the American colonies and later established offices in America that, along with offices established by Americans, grew during the nineteenth and early twentieth centuries in concert with increasing business and trade.

Public accounting, in which expert accountants offered their services to the public at large, is thought to have existed in England and America since early eighteenth century. References to public accountants in England date from 1720 when accountant Charles Snell provided a special report on the accounts of Sawbridge & Co. following the collapse of the South Sea Company of which Jacob Sawbridge was a director. In America, Browne Tymms has been recognized as the earliest known public accountant as a result of his 1718 advertisements in Boston newspapers indicating that he kept merchants' and shopkeepers' books (Previts and Merino, 1979, 8–9).

In England from 1773, *accomptant* or a similar title began to be listed in old city directories either for individuals or with others. The accomptant title was usually coupled with another specialty such as agent, broker, writing master, auctioneer, or appraiser, indicating that the occupation of public accountant needed to be supplemented with other duties. Littleton (1933, 267) notes that in all of the years from 1773 to 1800, there were only 60 such entries in the directories of major British cities. This indicates the slow growth of early public practice considering that the population of Great Britain exceeded 12 million in 1780 and 15 million in 1800. Only London passed the mark of 100 listings for accountants, with 210 accountants listed in 1845.

Until mid-nineteenth century, the work of public accountants can be said to have consisted of keeping accounts, preparing accounting reports, acting as a fiduciary, performing actuarial computations, and acting in bankruptcy liquidations. A very large part of their work was related to bankruptcy and fiduciary responsibilities. During the latter part of the century, the auditing of the books of limited liability companies increasingly added to the public accountants' scope of services.

Littleton cites a correspondent in *The Accountant* who "testifies to the fact that accountants were largely engaged in bankruptcy cases long before the acts of 1831 and 1849" (1933, 279). Between 1825 and 1883 there were seven bankruptcy statutes enacted. The 1825 act required accounts for all bankrupt property received and distributed. Public audits were made by commissioners in charge of bankruptcy liquidations. Later acts added provisions for accounting statements to be prepared by the bankrupt and presented to court officials. "It was regular practice to employ an accountant to insure correctness of the statements" (1973, 279).

The increasing demand for public accountants continued as the British Companies Acts during the late part of the nineteenth and early twentieth centuries established registration and other rules for limited liability companies. H. C. Edey evaluated the various acts between 1844 and 1947 (1982, 95). Before the 1844 act, corporations with limited liability were created by Royal charters or by special acts of Parliament. The Joint Stock Companies Act of 1844 allowed formation by simple registration of corporate entities with transferable stock and required companies to "keep books of account; to present a . . . balance sheet at each ordinary meeting of shareholders; to appoint auditors whose duty it would be to report on the balance sheet . . . and who were entitled to examine the books and question officers of the company" (95).

These provisions were eliminated in the Companies Act of 1856, not to be restored until 1900. Compulsory accounting and audits did continue to apply to parliamentary established corporations such as railroads, banks, and insurance companies during this period. And, it was increasingly common for audits to be performed on accounts of widely held stock companies.

The auditors envisioned in the companies acts of the mid to late nineteenth century were not the professional public accountants who were becoming more numerous as years went by, but the auditor was thought of as a layman who acted on behalf of shareholders, and who could, should he choose, employ public accountants at company expense. By 1900 the use of professional public accountants had, however, become widespread. In commenting upon events leading up to the act of 1900, Edey noted, "the professional auditor was by now an accepted part of the scene. There was indeed some support at the time for making an audit by professional accountants obligatory, but this measure was not destined to reach the Statute Book for another forty-seven years" (1956, 127).

The rising business and economic conditions and changes in the various companies acts during the nineteenth century placed new responsibilities on and gave new opportunities to the profession. Practitioners began to form professional accounting societies designed to assist members in taking advantage of the new opportunities and to protect the public and the profession in the performance of these duties. Scottish accountants organized and were granted a Royal warrant in 1854 for the first such professional society, using the name Society of Accountants in Edinburgh. In England, several professional groups had organized by 1877, and in 1880 these groups formed the Institute of Chartered Accountants of England and Wales, which had an original membership of 527 expanding to 1025 in 1881 (Littleton, 1933, 316). The stated purposes of the Institute were to foster members' professional practice and to regulate professional conduct. Admission was by examination only (266–70).

By 1905, Brown reported that there were an estimated 11,000 accountants who were members of professional societies in which "the United Kingdom accounts for half that number, Italy for one fourth, the British Colonies for 15 per cent., the United States for 5 per cent., and South America, Holland, Sweden, and Belgium for the remaining 5 per cent" (334).

The above discussions of the trends in the work of British accountants is supported by Previts' (1985, 23) study of the fees earned by the public accounting firm of Whinney, Smith and Whinney, a predecessor firm to Ernst and Young. In the earliest year studied, 1848, the firm earned 73 percent of fees for insolvency work, another 17 percent for trustee and executorship work, with but 1.9 percent for accounting. No fees were from auditing services. As late as 1880, the firm derived 72 percent of fees from insolvency with 3.5 percent from trustee and executorship work. Accounting work had by 1880 risen to 11.2 percent and auditing to 11 percent. In 1900, insolvency services remained important, bringing in approximately 20 percent of all fees. Trustee and executorship work was down to 5.6 percent. Accounting had grown to 17 percent and auditing to 53 percent of total fees. The latest year in which insolvency work was a major part of fees was 1925 with 27 percent from insolvency and 7.4 percent from trustee and executorship work. In that year, auditing fees were 48 percent and taxation work had grown to 5 percent of the total. From 1930 to 1960, the last year of the study, auditing fees were no less than 60 percent of the total of any year. Fees from taxation work gradually increased and from 1950 to 1960 were in the range of 11 percent to 14 percent of total fees.

Another interesting overview of the beginnings and evolution of British, and as it turns out, U.S. public accounting firms is provided in *The Accountant*, which published a series of articles titled "What's in a Name." Family trees of the largest public accounting firms in British practice in 1989 are traced to their beginnings (Boys, 1989; 1990). The oldest root firm listed in the series was Josiah Wade, established in 1780. All firms listed had roots extending back to the nineteenth century with the most recent year of establishment being 1875.

The study includes all of the largest U.S. accounting firms, until 1989 known as the Big Eight, because in 1989 they were all international partners of the British firms studied, clearly indicating that the roots of the largest international accounting firms are planted in both British and U.S. professions.

Early public accounting in the United States was in many ways intertwined with the British profession. British accountants, it seems certain, were dispatched to report on investments throughout colonial times. Early U.S. public accounting offices were generally established by British professionals or by those the British had trained. Previts and Merino (1979, 94) indicate that "British auditors had begun to reside in America as London firms found it less expensive to provide services on an extended basis by establishing resident offices in major U.S. cities. As business increased, the English firms were slowly Americanized."

Directory listings for accountants appeared as early as 1786 in the United States but were very few in number until late nineteenth century. New York is reported to have had 31 local practitioners listed as public accountants in 1880, 66 in 1890, and 183 in 1899. Chicago had only 3 local practitioners listed in 1880, 24 in 1890, and 71 in 1899 (Moyer, 1951, 4). A similar report of the number of early U.S. public accountants is given by Previts and Merino (1979, 90) who also report that Louisville, Kentucky, had 5 practicing accountants in 1885, indicating that public accountants were spread throughout the country even in medium-sized cities. In New York, Chicago, and Philadelphia public accountants totaled 81 in 1884 increasing to 322 by 1889. The first office of the British firm of Price, Waterhouse was opened in New York in 1890 with a Chicago office opened in 1892. Haskins and Sells was founded in New York in 1895 (Edwards, 1960, 50).

In these years prior to state C.P.A. legislation, the profession in the United States did not have specific legal recognition. Early professional societies conducted examinations and gave recognition to members as qualified accountants. The Institute of Accountants and Bookkeepers formed in 1882 and is thought to have been the first U.S. professional accounting society. The organization operated for 25 years. Its membership included many respected accountants. Members of the highest class of membership of the Institute were "required to pass examinations which were described as severe" (Edwards, 1960, 52). The American Association of Public Accountants was formed in 1886, became the American Institute of Accountants in 1916, and in 1957 was renamed the American Institute of Certified Public Accountants.

   Both of these professional groups were instrumental in passage of the first American certified public accountant legislation in New York state in 1896. This was the first legal recognition afforded the designation of certified public accountant (C.P.A.) in the United States. Other states rapidly followed and, by 1913, 31 states had passed C.P.A. legislation. A movement for federal C.P.A. regulation failed. Congress was reluctant to pass legislation that pertained to one profession and which might violate states' rights. The cumulative numbers of C.P.A. certificates issued increased from 56 in 1896 to 2,265 by 1913 and to 85,852 by 1958. Many of the early certificates were issued to existing expert practitioners by waiver rather than by examination (Edwards, 1960, 68–77, 363).

   These early laws provided for the issuance of C.P.A. certificates and restricted the right to express opinions regarding financial statements to C.P.A. holders in the various states. A number of court cases on the constitutionality of these provisions followed and, beginning with the upholding of the Wisconsin accountancy law in 1936, were held to be constitutional (Edwards, 1960, 174).

   With legal recognition by the states and as economic activity in America increased rapidly, the profession was in a position for expansion of services to meet the needs of decision makers during the years following 1900. Census data reflect the substantial growth in accounting services taking place over those years. From 1900 to 1970, while the gross national product measured in constant dollars grew by 9.4 times and the total population grew by 2.7 times, the number of accountants and auditors grew by nearly 31 times from 23,000 in 1900 to 712,000 in 1970. In terms of accountants and auditors as a percentage of the population, in 1900 only 1 in 3,300 was an accountant or auditor. This decreased steadily until, in 1970, 1 in 363 was an accountant or auditor. These data include all accountants and auditors whether in public practice or not.

   The increase in membership of the American Institute of Accountants perhaps more closely indicates the growth in public accounting. Membership of the American Institute of Accountants, the predecessor to the American Institute of Certified Public Accountants, was 1,150 in 1916 (Edwards, 1960, 117). Membership grew to 16,000 in 1950, 37,897 in 1960, 74,413 in 1970, 161,319 in 1980, and 218,855 in 1984 (Previts, 1985), and in 1989 stood at over 280,000 (Palmer, 1989, 84). The number of C.P.A.s in the United States was estimated at 39,000 in 1950, 59,000 in 1960, and 117,000 in 1970 (Previts and Merino, 1979, 305).

Among the important stimuli to the growth of accountants in general and public accountants in particular were the passage in 1909 of federal tax legislation that levied a franchise tax as a percentage of corporate income and the passage in 1913 of the sixteenth amendment to the constitution permitting taxation of income. These laws required many businesses and individuals who had not done so before to keep records of income. The effects of the income taxation, it seems certain, contributed greatly to the doubling of the number of accountants and auditors in the United States from 1910 to 1920. During World War I, high rates of taxation, a complex war revenue act, and excess profits tax all contributed to demand for accountants. The C.P.A. position was further enhanced when, in 1924, the Federal Board of Appeals held that certified public accountants as well as attorneys were qualified to appear before the board (Edwards, 1960, 101-9).

Federal securities acts passed in the aftermath of the stock market crash of 1929 provided public accountants with vastly expanded markets for their services. The passage of the Securities Act of 1933 and the Securities Exchange Act of 1934 established requirements and responsibilities for the independent audit of financial statements of corporations who issue corporate securities sold in interstate and foreign commerce. Great responsibilities were given auditors for performing the examinations necessary to form opinions about the financial statements that are required in both registration statements and periodic reports to the Securities and Exchange Commission.

The securities legislation coupled with income tax legislation laid the basis for the great rise of public accounting both in the United States and subsequently in the world at large. In 1932, *Fortune* (June 1932, 63) noted that "in 1886 the gross earnings of the twenty-five men who were professional public accountants did not exceed $250,000; today there are many thousands, with a gross income of some $60,000,000." *Fortune* provided a roster of "the chief accounting firms" that certified balance sheets for 700 companies whose securities were listed on the New York Stock Exchange. A perusal of the 1932 roster discloses that the same firms, or successors, remain today "the chief accounting firms" of the United States: Price, Waterhouse & Co.; Haskins & Sells; Ernst & Ernst; Peat, Marwick, Mitchell & Co.; Arthur Young & Co.; Lybrand, Ross Bros. & Montgomery; Touche, Niven & Co.; Arthur Andersen & Co.; Deloitte, Plender, Griffith & Co.; and Barrow Wade, Guthrie & Co.

In addition to substantial increases in tax and auditing work, management advisory services increased in tandem. A major part of the public accountant's business is the giving of advice on a wide range of problems, more or less connected to accounting. The C.P.A. is trained in accounting as it applies to business and other fields. The jobs of determining taxable income and conducting examinations to express opinions on financial statements require an in-depth knowledge and study of client organizations and environments in which clients operate. The public accounting firm, by the nature of its services, consists of individuals who have had much experience with a wide variety of problems confronted by clients. The accounting firms have been over the years a repository of experience and knowledge that clients have frequently found useful far beyond their accounting, attestation, and tax duties.

Following World War II, corporations, particularly U.S. corporations, began a global expansion unparalleled in history. Increased international ownership of corporate securities was part of the expansion. Accountants found that they needed to prepare worldwide accounting records and reports. Public accounting firms found that they needed to audit financial statements literally spanning the world to satisfy the needs of corporate clients and security owners and the requirements of world securities markets. The expression of audit opinions required adequate examinations in which sufficient, competent evidence was obtained. Audit service for large international companies required a large, professional organization with skilled, knowledgeable people acting in an independent and ethical manner and had geographically dispersed but centrally controlled facilities. In short, the expansion of U.S. and worldwide economic activity required accelerated development of accounting firms.

In the United States the public accounting profession in 1947 faced a rapidly expanding national economy. U.S. gross national product increased by 56 percent from $282 billion in 1947 to $440 billion in 1960. During the same period, annual total personal income increased by 110 percent; annual retail trade in dollars increased by 84 percent; annual number of new business incorporations increased by 62 percent; and the annual number of Securities and Exchange Commission registrations increased by 206 percent (Arthur Andersen & Company, 1963, 76).

Public accounting firms grew rapidly both nationally and internationally. Arthur Andersen, for example, increased the total number of clients from 2,300 in 1947 to 19,000 in 1963. The total number of offices was 17 with 848 personnel in 1947; it was expanded to 60 offices with 4,231 personnel in 1963. Prior to World War II, Arthur Andersen had relied upon overseas accounting firms for clients' international operations. International offices began to be added in the late 1940s and, by 1963, the firm had 27 offices outside the United States (Arthur Andersen & Company, 1963, 107).

There was similar growth in other public accounting firms during these years as the profession responded to the needs of their clients. Firms spread and grew through a combination of establishing new offices, buying practices of other firms, and merging practices.

Louis H. Penney (1961, 51–58) conducted a series of interviews with managing partners of the Big Eight accounting firms and others. He reported that "one result of this tidal wave of diversification and dispersal of business has been a great upsurge in the number of nationwide and world-wide audits." He also suggested that "as a corollary, the large accounting firms that have been serving these expanding companies have been obliged to enlarge their organizations and to follow their clients into new territories." The primary topic of Penney's interviews was accounting firm mergers. Merger activities were accelerating. Firms canvassed by Penney reported that in 1946–1955, 50 mergers had taken place compared with 113 mergers during 1956–1961. Many reasons were given for the mergers. "The most compelling reason, offered more than half the time, is to protect or retain clients" (53). Accounting firms needed to expand to meet growing client requirements for services. This was seen to be particularly true of management services. As corporate clients grew, particularly when they grew internationally, smaller public accounting firms could not offer the depth or breadth of expertise needed by clients.

The "chief accounting firms of America" listed by *Fortune* in 1932 were in an excellent position to continue their growth as corporations grew larger. Arther M. Louis (1968, 178) reported that by 1968 "the accounting profession is dominated by eight large firms . . . which among them audit about 80 percent of the publicly held companies in the U.S." The list consisted of Peat, Marwick, Mitchell & Co.; Arther Andersen & Co.; Ernst & Ernst; Price Waterhouse & Co.; Haskins & Sells; Lybrand, Ross Bros. & Montgomery; Touche, Ross, Bailey & Smart; and Arthur Young & Company. These firms audited 96 percent of the largest 100 U.S. industrial companies and 94 percent of the largest 500 industrial companies. All of the Big Eight firms were reported to be heavily engaged in management consulting and tax services that accounted for about 40 percent of aggregate gross revenues. All were reported to have international operations. *Fortune* estimated that "the Big Eight are doing slightly more than two and a half times as much volume as they did in 1960" (178).

The extent of the Big Eight's international operations by 1978 is reflected in a *Forbes* report by Bob Tamarkin (November 27, 1978, 37) that lists estimates of Big Eight worldwide and U.S. revenues.

Worldwide revenues in 1978 exceeded $500 million for each of four firms with revenue of the remaining each above $400 million. Coopers & Lybrand, the name of Lybrand, Ross Bros. & Montgomery since a 1957 merger, topped the list at $595 million in revenue with Peat Marwick, Mitchell & Co. a close second with $586 million. Domestic U.S. revenues for four of the firms was between $200 and $300 million; three firms were between $300 and $400; and one firm, Peat Marwick, Mitchell & Co., topped $400 in U.S. revenue.

Previts (1985, 137) reported the distribution of fees of the Big Eight between 1977 and 1984 in service categories of audit, tax, and management advisory services. The proportion of total fees generated by audit service declined in all eight firms. In 1977, the highest percentage for audit was 79 percent of fees for Deloitte, Haskins & Sells, the name for Haskins & Sells since a 1978 merger, and the lowest was 61 percent for Peat Marwick Mitchell. By 1984 Deloitte, Haskins & Sells still had the highest percentage from audit at 68 percent while Arthur Andersen had the lowest with 50 percent. Tax service fees over the 1977 to 1984 period increased by a relatively small percentage for all firms. The largest increase was for Arthur Young from 19 percent in 1977 to 25 percent in 1984. Management advisory services increased in seven of the firms: Arthur Andersen from 19 percent in 1977 to 28 percent in 1984; Coopers and Lybrand from 12 percent to 13 percent; Deloitte, Haskins & Sells from 5 percent to 11 percent; Ernst & Whinney, the name for Ernst & Ernst since a 1979 merger, from 12 percent to 17 percent; Peat Marwick Mitchell from 11 percent to 17 percent; Price Waterhouse from 7 percent to 14 percent; Arthur Young from 11 percent to 14 percent. At Touche Ross, the name for Touche, Ross, Bailey & Smart since a 1969 merger, management advisory services remained the same in both years at 14 percent.

Since World War II, the increasing size of economies has required accounting firms of substantially increasing size. Operating in open markets and serving a widely dispersed set of owners and other third parties, the United States and United Kingdom accounting professions have been in an excellent position for rapid growth internationally.

U.S. and U.K. accounting and financial reports are geared to the needs of the widely dispersed and varied holders of securities. Rules and procedures of financial accounting, auditing, and reporting have been largely controlled by the accounting professions themselves, as opposed to a governmental body. Standard setters in both the United States and the United Kingdom are subjected to and respond to market forces as they set and uphold standards. Operating in this kind of an environment,

U.S. and U.K. accounting firms are well-suited and well-equipped to compete and to grow internationally as demand for their worldwide services grows.

The U.S. and British accounting firms have in fact come through their international firm affiliations and mergers to dominate world public accounting markets. Within the United States this dominance is virtually complete. In other areas of the world, firms not affiliated with the Big Eight have a substantial portion of the market.

Evidence that supports this view was developed at the Center for International Financial Analysis & Research in Princeton, New Jersey. Vinod B. Bavishi (1989) directed a study of 13,000 non-U.S. and 3,600 U.S. company financial statements. Of these financial statements, 67 percent were for 1987; 36 percent were for 1986. As a measure of company size, dollar equivalent sales for nonfinancial companies and dollar equivalent total assets for financial companies were summed across sampled companies.

The study found that within the United States, the Big Eight firms audited 94 percent of the 3,600 sampled companies. The U.S. client companies had 99 percent of total U.S. sales/asset dollars. In sampled non-U.S. companies, the Big Eight international accounting firms audited 62 percent of the companies that represented 75 percent of total sales/asset dollars.

The next largest eight international accounting firms, by comparison, audited 4 percent of the U.S. companies representing 1 percent of total sales/asset dollars and 8 percent of the non-U.S. companies representing 5 percent of sales/asset dollars. Auditing firms not affiliated with the big 16 audited 2 percent of the U.S. companies. Nonaffiliated accounting firms audited 30 percent of the non–U.S. companies, which had 20 percent of the sales/asset dollars.

In the developing countries, the presence of auditors not affiliated with the big 16 firms is higher than in the industrialized world. In the industrial nations sampled, 21 percent of all companies are audited by non-big sixteen international accounting firms. In developing countries, this jumps to a healthy 33 percent. Nonetheless, the Big Eight firms are dominant across the globe. The Bavishi study indicates that 84 percent of the top 1,000 multinational firms in his sample were audited by the Big Eight and 76 percent of the non-multinational companies sampled were audited by the Big Eight. When client companies were broken into industry groups, the Big Eight audits at least 75 percent of all companies within each group, based on total sales/asset dollars. The larger the size category, the greater the number of clients audited by the Big Eight.

To carry out their work, the international accounting firms can be found throughout the world. In 1988, the largest 16 international accounting firms had offices in 142 countries (Bavishi, 1989). They maintained a total of 5,567 offices with 31,751 partners, distributed over the globe as follows:

	Offices	Partners
Africa/Middle East	512	1,706
Asia/Pacific	762	3,870
Europe	2,122	10,233
North America	1,841	14,886
South America/Caribbean	330	1,056

The international accounting firms maintained 4,270 offices with 27,566 partners in industrial countries. In developing countries, they maintained 1,270 offices with 4,185 partners.

The international firms have grown steadily. From 1982 to 1988, worldwide total offices increased by 29 percent and the total number of partners increased by 38 percent. Within the United States, the number of offices increased by 11 percent and the number of partners by 29 percent. Substantially more growth took place outside the United States as the number of offices increased by 36 percent and the number of partners increased by 45 percent. In advanced industrial countries, offices of the international accounting firms grew by 26 percent and partners grew by 34 percent. In developing countries, offices increased 39 percent while partners increased by 72 percent (Bavishi, 1989).

Growth rates from the five-year period 1982 to 1987 in the numbers of partners worldwide of the top accounting firms provides another gauge of the rapid increases these firms are experiencing: Arthur Andersen, 30 percent; Arthur Young, 38 percent; Coopers & Lybrand, 44 percent; Deloitte, Haskins & Sells, 5.6 percent; Ernst & Whinney, 68 percent; KMG, 24 percent; Peat Marwick, 27 percent; Price Waterhouse, 28 percent; and Touche Ross, 32 percent. Average increase in partners for the 12 largest international firms was reported as 31 percent worldwide during this five-year period. In Europe growth was even larger. Partners in these same firms grew by 42 percent in Europe during 1982–1987 (Wyman, 1989).

Merging of practices seems to have long been a major growth strategy by which most of the world's largest C.P.A. firms came to dominance and by which they maintain their dominance. Mergers have been prevalent throughout the history of both British and U.S. accounting firms.

As discussed earlier in this chapter, Peter Boys in his series of *Accountancy* articles titled "What's in a Name" traced the names of accounting firms through a maze of mergers from 1880 to 1989. Circa 1880, British public accountants were either practicing on their own or in small partnerships. The largest firm at that time had 6 partners. British companies legislation in 1844 limited partnership size to 25 partners. This was decreased to 20 partners in 1856 legislation. The limitation on partnership size was repealed in 1967. Boys notes that although British accounting firm growth was restricted particularly in the later years, the restrictive laws could be circumvented by partnerships working in associations with cross or working agreements. The repeal of the limitation led to an immediate increase in size of partnerships, much of which came through mergers. "Today there are 15 firms with over 100 UK partners and one firm, Peat Marwick McLintock, with 514" (Boys, 1989, 100). Unimpeded by the British legislation's restriction, U.S. firms expanded throughout their histories through internal growth and mergers with other accounting firms.

Mergers continue to be a major source of growth both within nations and on an international scale with 40 reported in 1985, 46 in 1987, and 55 in 1988. The number of mergers from 1982 to 1988 included 34 in the United States, 21 in Japan, 18 in Canada, 15 in Australia, and 14 in the United Kingdom. During that period, international firms expanding the most actively were: KPMG Peat Marwick with 32 mergers; Touche Ross, 28; Deloitte, Haskins & Sells, 22; Price Waterhouse, 18; and Ernst & Whinney, 17. One of the 32 mergers for KPMG was the merger of Peat Marwick Mitchell with KMG Main Hurdman in 1987. Klynveld Main Goerdeler-Main Hurdman had itself been formed through merger in 1979 of firms from West Germany, the Netherlands, Britain, Canada, Australia, and the United States.

Prior to the merger of Peat Marwick and KMG, Larry D. Horner, chairman of Peat, was quoted in *The Wall Street Journal* (Berton, 1986, 6). "The synergy we generate will enable us to target big clients in every major business area of the world." The merged firms increased Peat's European offices sixfold and doubled its African and Far Eastern offices.

The AICPA estimates that in 1989 there were a total of between 40,000 and 45,000 C.P.A. firms in the United States with approximately 30,000 operating as sole practitioners. Of the total AICPA membership in 1989, 130,000 were in public practice. One-fourth of these were employed by the top 25 firms (Palmer, 1989, 84). "The profession's growth has left us with eight major firms, an expanding number of small firms and a declining number of midsized firms" (85). Palmer found public accounting "as opposed to some other CPA firm product lines" to be mature. "As a profession, it exhibits characteristics typical of mature industries — slow growth, intense price competition, lower profit margins, a lack of product differentiation on the part of customers and shakeout of marginal competitors" (85).

Since then, Arthur Young and Ernst & Whinney have merged to form Ernst & Young. Deloitte, Haskins & Sells have merged with Touche Ross to form Deloitte & Touche. The combined revenues in 1986 of Ernst & Young were estimated at $1.55 billion in the United States and $2.7 billion worldwide; for Deloitte and Touche at $1.2 billion in the United States and $2.2 billion worldwide; these combinations are in the general category with Peat Marwick, which had estimated U.S. revenues of $1.4 billion and worldwide revenues of $2.7 billion (Berton, 1986, 3). In a later prediction, the Deloitte and Touche combination was predicted to create a firm with annual 1989 U.S. revenues of close to $2 billion and worldwide revenue of more than $4 billion (*Wall Street Journal*, August 14, 1989, A4). This compares with estimates for KPMG Peat Marwick revenue in 1989 of $1.84 billion in the United States and $3.9 billion worldwide (Berton, 1989a, A5A). Berton (1989b, A6) suggested that "over the long run . . . it's possible that the merged firms could better serve their clients . . . because the mergers will fill in geographic and service gaps and weaknesses, and will pool capital needed to provide . . . expensive consulting services."

2

Major International Differences in Accounting Standards

Even though commerce and economic activities have long been conducted across national borders, accounting activities until recently have largely centered within the nation-state. Accounting services have grown in response to information needs focused primarily within individual nations. Standards for accounting, auditing, and financial reporting have been and continue to be set almost exclusively by nations presumably in response to perceived needs for accounting and financial information within the nation-state. These perceived needs and the resulting accounting are affected by national attributes that many believe are dependent upon social, cultural, political, and economic aspects of the nation-state.

In recent decades great increases in international trade and business fostered by innovations in transportation and communication interlinking large parts of the world have made the focus of many business activities that were formerly centered in one or another nation-state at least in part truly global in scope. World-spanning business organizations have been rapidly evolving and expanding. Evidence of greatly increasing international economic activity and integration is substantial.

Some view the future as a "borderless world" (Ohmae, 1990) in which economies will be interlinked in a "wave of economic and intellectual interdependence of nations" (216). Kenichi Ohmae discusses current developments toward a borderless world. "An isle is emerging that is bigger than a continent — The Inter-linked Economy of the Triad (the United States, Europe, and Japan), joined by aggressive economies such as Taiwan, Hong Kong, and Singapore" (x). He indicates that the interlinked triad economy "is becoming so powerful that it has swallowed most consumers and corporations, made traditional national borders almost disappear, and pushed bureaucrats, politicians, and the military toward the status of declining industries" (xi).

In this integrating world environment, accounting is called upon to continue its adaptions to facilitate ever-wider needs of decision makers. J. M. Samuels and A. G. Piper (1985, 30) observed that "the accounting practices in a country are continually changing. The direction in which they move depends on internal economic changes within the country and upon outside influences." Chapter 1 discussed how accountants and accounting services have changed reflecting changing human development and economic conditions. The progress of the adaptation of accounting, auditing, and financial reporting standards and the apparent directions of these adaptations to meet the challenges of the future borderless world are the subjects of this chapter.

Statistics for the United States indicate the growing dimensions of world trade. U.S. annual imports from 1936 to 1940 averaged $3.2 billion, while annual exports averaged $2.5 billion. Average annual exports grew to $10.1 billion by 1941–1945; to $11.8 billion by 1946–1950; and to $15.3 billion by 1951–1955. Average annual imports grew to $3.5 billion in 1941–1945; to $6.7 billion in 1946–1950; and to $10.8 billion in 1951–1955 (U.S. Bureau of the Census, 1960). By 1960, exports were $19.6 billion and imports $15.0 billion. By 1970, annual exports had grown by 1.17 times and imports by 1.67 times over 1960 averages. Exports by 1980 had grown by over 4 times and imports by over 5 times 1970 totals. And by 1988, annual U.S. exports stood at $322 billion and imports at $441 billion. Annual exports had grown by 16 times and imports by 29 times from 1960 to 1988 (U.S. Bureau of the Census, 1990).

The interdependency of nations is further evidenced by worldwide statistical estimates. Total worldwide merchandise trade across national borders in 1988 was estimated to have increased to a total of $2.9 trillion from $2 trillion in 1980. World trade growth in volume terms also reached a record level. The Organization for Economic Cooperation and Development (OECD) estimated that world trade volume increased by 9 percent in 1988 from a 5.8 percent pace in 1987. Trade in business services in 1988 was reported to be $580 billion or one-fifth the size of world merchandise trade (International Trade Administration, 1989, 3–6).

International direct investment has grown substantially. The outward worldwide stock of direct investments abroad reached an estimated $599 billion in 1984, nearly a ninefold increase over the $68 billion estimated for 1960. The percentages of the world's stock of outward direct investment in 1984 was reported as follows: United States, 43 percent; Europe, 44 percent; Japan, 4 percent; Canada, 4 percent; other developed countries, 1 percent; developing countries, 3 percent. The percentages of the world's stock of inward direct investments was reported as Europe, 30 percent; United States, 27 percent; developing countries, 26 percent; Canada, 10 percent; other developed countries, 7 percent (1988, ii).

The growth in global financial markets is described by Michael R. Sesit, Ann Monroe, and Peter Truell (1986, 29D). "In myriad ways and with dazzling speed hundreds of billions of dollars pour into one account and out of another around the world, around the clock." They go on to say: "The unending flow of money greases the machinery of the international financial markets as never before. It enables borrowers to find funds and lenders to seek the best return for their assets." The fast pace of innovation in financial markets has raised concerns that national regulators and participating financial institutions themselves cannot effectively manage their fast-paced changes.

Great changes in world financial markets began with the emergence two decades ago of the Eurodollar market that created unregulated borrowing and lending. The value of Eurodollar market issues increased rapidly and by 1986 stood at an estimated $3 trillion. This huge market provided the impetus for the deregulation of domestic financial markets around the world, giving explosive growth throughout the 1970s and 1980s to worldwide financial markets. These world-spanning markets were made possible by advances in telecommunications, floating exchange rates, deregulation of currency controls, and deregulation of flows of capital across many national borders. Indicative of the dimensions of the financial flows are the estimates for daily cash payment transaction totals that were reported in 1986 to average $1.1 trillion, an increase from $175 billion in 1974 (Sesit, Monroe, and Truell, 1986, 40D). These flows of cash are so large that it seems virtually impossible for national authorities to maintain control.

The growth in international equity markets was discussed by Larry D. Horner (1986, 5). "On the equity side, we are rapidly moving toward a 24-hour global market in which investors in New York or Tokyo or London will be able to trade any major stock at any hour of the day or night." Further, Horner points out that "one of the biggest changes is the growth of the electronic off-exchange market — where foreign share volume has been averaging between $200 billion and $300 billion a day." Electronic markets offered by the London exchange's quote system and NASDAC have "raised the number of trans-Atlantic price quotes to nearly 600, and will probably push daily off-exchange volume a lot closer to the billion-dollar mark."

Much of the global expansion in equity trading has bypassed the organized stock exchanges. Foreign stocks listed on major world stock exchanges have not kept pace. *Euromoney* reported in 1986 that "foreign listings on seven major stock exchanges have increased by only about 3% over the past two years, on a net basis, to reach 1,439 at the end of September" (43). The numbers of foreign equity listings on the seven major exchanges were London, 505; Amsterdam, 278; Zurich, 196; Frankfurt, 189; Paris, 180; New York, 58; and Tokyo, 33 (*Euromoney*, 1986, 43). By March 1989, foreign equity as compared to total stocks listed on six of these exchanges increased somewhat: London, 595 of 2656; Amsterdam, 291 of 572; Zurich, 1105 of 2914; Frankfurt, 329 of 741; Paris, 222 of 888; and New York, 74 of 1681 (*Institutional Investor*, 1989, 197–204). Zurich and Frankfurt foreign stock listings increased substantially, but the other major exchanges added relatively few new foreign listings.

Euromoney (1986, 43) reported, "There are a number of factors that explain the apparent reluctance to list, including the cost and the sometimes onerous requirements involved, such as disclosure and the use of different accounting methods." The main factor, in *Euromoney*'s view, "is that technology has made the traditional concept of a national trading floor redundant. To have its shares traded, a company no longer has to be listed; it only has to be on a system of some kind" (43).

Despite rapidly changing global conditions in international business and financial markets, accounting and auditing standards remain by and large the preserve of national jurisdictions. Substantial differences remain in national financial reporting practices and resultant company financial statements from country to country. There have been movements toward harmonization of differing national standards by some regional and world organizations. These are ongoing developments, the results of which remain to be seen.

Nations have used several patterns of regulating accounting services within their jurisdictions. A public and private approach is used by some nations in which private professional organizations set standards that often are overseen by a national authority. In other countries standards are set by governmental authorities directly by law or indirectly through government bodies. In some countries standards are geared to taxation, central planning, or other governmental aims. Still other countries have a mixture of these approaches.

The differing processes of setting national accounting standards were studied by Robert Bloom and M. S. Naciri in nine countries: the United States, Canada, England, West Germany, Australia, New Zealand, Sweden, Japan, and Switzerland. Each country, they observed, had a different structure and different procedures for setting standards. Bloom and Naciri attribute these to differing cultures and traditions. "The social, political, and economic environments in these countries can explain differences in their standard setting processes" (1989, 92). West Germany, for example, sets standards by law. Japanese standards are set by governmental bodies. In the other seven countries studied by Bloom and Naciri, a private and public approach is taken.

A number of works exist that have detailed the approaches taken by various countries.[1] These studies also suggest that differences in social, political, and economic environments are root causes of differing accounting and reporting systems.

Geoffrey S. Arpan and Lee H. Radebaugh (1985, 13–40) use a conceptual framework for analyzing business practices developed by Farmer and Richman (1966). The framework organizes environmental characteristics into four major groups: educational, sociological, economic groups, each with nine characteristics, and a political and legal group with six characteristics. Arpan and Radebaugh use the framework in a broad fashion to discuss how accounting in various countries is affected, observing that all the environmental factors need to be considered when analyzing a country's accounting system (24). "In effect, these characteristics become constraints on a firm's ability to operate effectively and efficiently . . . explain the way business organizations in a particular country operate and, to a certain extent, make it possible to predict how they will operate in a given situation" (13). These authors state that behavior, or accounting standards, in a given country should be "judged in terms of its own cultural context, and not from that of an outsider" (15).

Ahmed Belkaoui (1985, 28–49) comments in some depth on this point, seeing the determinants of national differences in accounting as cultural relativism (29). Accounting concepts and the reporting and disclosure system in any given country are influenced by cultural, linguistic, political, economic, and demographic characteristics and legal and tax environments in that country. A country's accounting standards and practices should be judged and understood in the context of that country and not another.

An early description of the many divergent accounting practices and standards then extant in the world was given in 1911 by Hatfield (1966) who discussed the many ways in which accounting practices and standards varied among the countries of England, France, Germany, and the United States. Hatfield noted, "It is a delicate task to attempt to characterize the accounting systems of the different countries or to make comparisons which might seem invidious" (180).

With the many differing sets of standards, it is not surprising that a number of classification methods have been proposed over the years to group countries with similar standards.[2] Some of these studies base classification on national environmental factors. Others have used accounting standards themselves to group and classify nations. Some have made a distinction between accounting standards for valuation and accounting standards of disclosure. All bear out the fact that national standards vary substantially from country to country.

An early classification system was prepared by George C. Watt, Richard M. Hammer, and Marianne Burge (1977), Price Waterhouse partners with long international accounting experience, who evaluated the likelihood that information in financial statements "prepared for use in a foreign country and reported upon by a reputable local (as opposed to international) accounting firm" would be viewed as presented fairly by U.S. readers (186–87). The authors acknowledge that their comparisons were highly subjective and were intended only as a guide. They used several criteria to classify 45 countries in comparison with the United States. Was there a general standard of fair presentation recognized in the particular country? To what extent were standards defined by law or practice? What was the extent of differences from U.S. principles? Are the country's practices unfavorably influenced by tax laws? Was there an organized and active accounting profession?

This resulted in 6 categories. Spain and Switzerland were thought to have statutory requirements that did not approach U.S. standards. In 11 countries, tax legislation was the predominant influence on standards.[3] Fair presentation was found in principle but not in practice in 7 countries.[4] In 3 countries, Chile, Germany, and Japan, standards approach those of the United States but some valuation principles used would not be acceptable in the United States. In 5 countries, Bahamas, Barbados, Nigeria, Panama, and Trinidad & Tobago, standards were based on U.S., U.K., or Canadian standards. Finally, 17 countries were thought to have standards "broadly equivalent to the U.S." (Watt, Hammer, and Burge, 1977, 187) although minor differences still occurred.[5] The authors noted that financial reporting in the various countries "is a constantly changing picture with a number of recent favorable trends since 1974" (186). Arpan and Radebaugh, commenting upon the fact that only 45 countries were evaluated by Watt, Hammer, and Burge, suggested that inclusion of the other 100 or so countries of the world would have resulted in a much larger total for countries not approaching U.S. standards than the total for all the other categories combined (1985, 330).

Several accounting practices studies have used data from Price Waterhouse accounting principles surveys. R. C. DaCosta, J. C. Bourgeois, and W. M. Lawson (1978) used cluster analysis on data from Price Waterhouse's 1973 *Survey of Accounting Principles in 38 Countries*. Data for the 38 countries were clustered using 100 accounting practices that produced two classification groups. One included the United Kingdom and nine former members of the British Empire; the other classification group had the United States, France, Germany, and all other countries except Canada and the Netherlands, which were thought by these researchers to be unclassifiable. A two-group classification system for the 38 countries involved would appear to be relatively useless. The group that contains the United States and all other countries does not appear valid in comparison to what is known about varying accounting principles in countries of the world.

Using 1973 and 1975 Price Waterhouse survey data, R. D. Nair and W. G. Frank (1980) concluded that classification of countries into groups based on accounting measurement practices would not result in the same groupings of countries as classification based on disclosure practices. This suggests that the groupings of countries in classification systems depends upon which accounting attribute is used as a basis for classification. Further analysis was made that concluded that the same "underlying environmental variables (such as the structure of the economy and trading affiliations of each country)" (426) were not associated with the two groupings obtained by classifying on measurement versus disclosure practices. The researchers found that the specific environmental variables most closely associated with each subset were different.

The classifications by measurement practices resulted in four groups: a British Commonwealth model with 14 countries; a Latin American model with 10 countries; a continental European model with 8 countries; and a United States model with 6 countries.

Christopher Nobes (1983) reviewed the Price Waterhouse data finding it flawed by "straight-forward mistakes, misleading answers, swamping of important questions by trivial ones, and exaggeration of the differences between the USA and the UK because of the familiarity of these countries (and thus their differences) to the compilers of the survey questions" (2). As to the studies based on the Price Waterhouse data, Nobes observed that the data may not be appropriate for the purposes used because "the surveys report not on actual practices but on what practices might be if non-mandatory rules were obeyed or on what Price Waterhouse partners might like practices to be" (21). In the studies reviewed, cluster analysis had been used that did "not directly test a particular hypothetical classification. It classifies a mass of data that was not collected with this purpose in mind" (21).

Nobes suggested and tested a classification system for developed western countries (Nobes and Parker, 1981; Nobes, 1983) based on his own knowledge and the comments of other experts. In this model of financial reporting practices, countries are first broken into *Micro-based* and *Macro-uniform* classes. Under *Micro-based* are subclasses of *Business Economics Theory*, which contains only the Netherlands, and *Business Practice Pragmatic British Origin*, which is further broken into two subclasses, the *U.K. Influenced* and the *U.S. Influenced*. Under *U.K. Influenced* are listed New Zealand, Australia, Ireland, and the U.K. Under *U.S. Influenced* are listed Canada and the United States. The *Macro-Uniform* class has two subclasses of *Government Economics* with only Sweden listed under it, and the *Continental: Government, Tax, Legal* which has two further subclasses: *Tax-based* and *Law-based*. Listed in the *Tax-based* group are Italy, France, Belgium, and Spain. In the *Law-based* are West Germany and Japan (Nobes, 1986, 25). This classification system appears to be in line with what is known of accounting practices in studied countries.

Another classification method by Gerhard G. Mueller, Helen Gernon, and Gary Meek (1991, 11–19) suggests that the attributes affecting financial accounting development in a country are the relationship between business organizations and providers of capital, political and economic ties with other countries, legal systems, levels of inflation, size and complexity of business enterprises, sophistication of management and the financial community, and general levels of education. These authors make three groupings: a British-American model, a continental model and a South American model.

In British-American model countries, accounting is oriented toward decision needs of investors and creditors. These countries have large developed securities markets in which business raises large amounts of capital. Education levels are high and users of financial information are sophisticated. They also have large, multinational corporations. There are 43 countries listed under the British-American model.

In continental model countries, businesses have close ties to their banks, which supply most capital needs. Financial accounting is legalistic and tends to be highly conservative. Accounting is not oriented toward decision needs of capital providers but is designed for government needs in income taxation or macroeconomic reporting. There are 27 countries listed under the continental model.

The South American model includes most countries in South America where there has been persistent use of adjustments for inflation. Accounting is oriented toward needs of government planning. Uniform practices are imposed on businesses. Tax-basis accounting is often used for financial reporting purposes. There are 9 countries listed under the South American model (Mueller, Gernon, and Meek, 1991, 16).

These authors see two emerging models. An Islamic model has a theological base and prohibits recognition of interest on money. An International Standards model arises from international efforts at the harmonization of financial accounting "especially for multinational corporations and international financial markets participants" (Mueller, Gernon, and Meek, 1991, 18).

Commenting on political changes in 1989 and 1990 in Communist bloc nations, the authors note that accounting orientations in these command economies may change in due course. Currently, "financial accounting per se does not exist; what we refer to as **managerial accounting** comes closer to the Communist block accounting cluster" (Mueller, Gernon, and Meek, 1991, 19).

A study of financial statements of 1,000 industrial companies from 24 countries led Frederick D. S. Choi and Vinod B. Bavishi (1983) to conclude, "Contrary to what is normally presumed, fundamental differences in national accounting principles, as gleaned from the reporting practices of the world's leading industrial companies, aren't that great" (68). The study compared the treatment by large companies in 23 countries to that used by large U.S. companies for 32 different accounting principles. There was a total of 736 possible observations that could have been reported. Of these, 69 were "not found" and 4 were reported as "not applicable." A total of 254 differences were reported from U.S. principles, or 38 percent of the total possible differences of 663. Of the 32 principles there was only one for which no differences were reported for any of the 23 countries. For 12 of the principles, there were 10 or more countries where principles used differed from those of the United States. The authors noted that "major differences appear to revolve around such issues as consolidation and accounting for goodwill, deferred taxes, long-term leases, discretionary reserves, inflation, and foreign exchange translation gains and losses" (68). The principles in these categories accounted for about two-thirds of the 254 observed differences.

Auditing standards in the various nations of the world are also divergent. The basis for legal requirement for independent audits rests on public interest and results from limited liability granted to corporations.

Behind the legal requirement is the necessity to have independent verification for accountability purposes when economic resources owned by private parties or in which the public has an interest are controlled by others. Audit of financial statements is seen to be useful by many because of the credibility added. Leslie G. Campbell notes, "This added usefulness is derived from the reduction in the risk to the user groups that the financial statements may include materially distorted information" (1985, 11).

Regulation of auditing and financial reporting is country specific. Specifics of requirements vary literally on a country-by-country basis. They range from the impressive standards of the developed countries to few (if any) requirements in many developing countries.

The divergence of national reporting and audit requirements were examined by Watt, Hammer, and Burge (1977) who reviewed published material in 1975 from 45 countries and categorized the countries into four groups based upon a comparison of general audit requirements in each country against U.S. requirements (214–15). Countries in the first group, 19 in number, required financial statements of all or most public companies to be examined by independent public accountants.[6] In the second group of 8, companies must appoint statutory examiners, and some companies, because of size, type of business, or sale of securities to the public, must be examined by independent public accountants.[7] In the third group of 9 countries, companies must appoint statutory examiners that need not be independent public accountants.[8] In the fourth group, with 9 countries, there were no audit requirements except for a limited number of companies such as banks, insurance companies, and other listed companies.[9] The authors note that categories are based on "general type of audit requirements in the 45 countries for the form of business organization most closely resembling a U.S. corporation. Other forms of business entities may be subject to the same or less stringent requirements" (214). The authors indicated that they made "no representation as to the degree of comparison between local auditing standards and auditing standards generally accepted in the United States" (214).

A 1986 reference work of national auditing and reporting requirements compiled by Peat, Marwick, Mitchell & Co. (1986) included general descriptions of requirements in 97 countries. Substantial progress since 1977 is apparent when requirements for countries listed in the second, third, and fourth groupings of the Watt, Hammer and Burge study are updated to 1986 with the Peat Marwick information.

From the second group, Argentina, Brazil, Japan, Mexico, Norway, Sweden, and Venezuela appear by 1986 to have improved their general audit requirements to a basis comparable with that of the United States and therefore should be in group one. Of the original countries, only Greece would remain in the second group, which was defined to include countries in which companies must appoint statutory examiners and in which some companies, because of size, type of business, or sale of securities to the public, must be examined by independent public accountants. Italy appears also in 1986 to fall within the requirements of the second group rather than group three.

From group three, Belgium, Chile, France, Lebanon, and Switzerland appeared to meet the requirements for group one in 1986. Guatemala and Honduras appear to have fallen to group four, which is defined to include countries with no audit requirements except for limited types of companies such as banks and insurance companies. Bolivia and Panama appear to meet the requirements for group one. The remaining countries from the original group four appear not to have improved their audit requirements.[10] Nicaragua is not listed in the Peat Marwick inventory.

Thus, group one in 1986 contains 33 of the original 45 countries. Group two contains 2. Group three contains 1. Group four contains 8, or 9 if Nicaragua is included. These improvements in a span of a decade represent good and rather rapid progress.

Traditionally, accounting has evolved rather slowly. This slow pace of change should be expected as many forces in the economic, cultural, social, political, and legal environments of nations greatly influence accounting development. Since environments do differ from country to country, it is possible that differing accounting standards adequately reflect economic transactions and fulfill information needs in the particular environment. This would seem to be justification for the many and varied national standards in use. Unfortunately, this diversity, however much it may be justified within national jurisdictions, results in a lack of comparability from country to country causing, it would seem, diseconomies and increasing costs. Mueller, Gernon, and Meek (1991, 42) point out, "unfortunately, this diversity of accounting practice results in a general lack of comparability in financial reports from one country to the next."

With the rapid rise of multinational companies, the information needs of decision makers have rapidly transcended national boundaries. Accounting standards of the multinational company's native country are no longer the only standards that must be used in its financing and investing activities. The standards of the native country may not, in fact, be adequate at all for a world-spanning business.

The greatly increasing volume and variety of international business transactions have created market-driven needs for harmonization of accounting standards so that comparable information can be used across international borders. Arthur Wyatt states that "securities commissioners in many countries have come to recognize the improved efficiencies that would flow from elimination of accounting differences across countries." Further, he states, "Many believe that markets extract a price for these inefficiencies and that, therefore, financing costs would decline as inefficiencies related to accounting differences are eliminated" (1989, 107).

The task to reduce differences among the various national standards has been viewed by some as a process of standardization versus a process of harmonization. This view is described by Jeffrey S. Arpan and Lee H. Radebaugh (1985). "In a strict sense, standardization seeks to *eliminate* such differences by developing uniform standards, whereas harmonization seeks to *lessen* but not eliminate the differences, and to make differences more reconcilable with each other" (344).

Mark A. Holtzblatt and Samuel Fox (1983) view the dilemma as uniformity versus harmonization. They describe the present situation as diversity where each nation or area has its own principles and standards, that is, its own generally accepted accounting principles. They state: "International accounting writers and accountants agree that the existing diversity of accounting practices within the world community is undesirable" (43). They define uniformity as the situation in which all nations of the world would be governed by a common set of accounting standards. Uniformity could mean "a rigid code which allows little flexibility or judgement on the part of the accountant." They view a second meaning as "a single body of rules governing world accounting practice similar to generally accepted accounting principles in the United States" (43). Under harmonization of international accounting principles, each country might have its own set of principles and standards but would cooperate with other countries to reduce "the friction created by diverse practices" (44). There might be, for example, multiple sets of statements for shareholders in various countries. Given the barriers to uniformity, Holtzblatt and Fox believe that harmonization seems to be the approach with best future prospects.

Irving L. Fantl (1971) rejects uniformity as "the solution . . . too simple and the problem too complex." He cautions, "however desirable such a monolithic concept appears, practical impediments to such uniformity must be clearly recognized" (13). He suggests, "increased international cooperation among accountants and an emphasis on reconciling existing accounting differences may be the most productive approach" (13). Fantl points out the problems within the United States in arriving at consensus on accounting matters. "If one well-organized professional group cannot reach agreement on basic procedures, how much more difficult will it be to establish world standards" (13).

Consensus seems to indicate that harmonization offers the best hope to achieving adequately comparable international accounting, auditing, and financial reporting. A governmental approach on a world basis seems out of the question given that there is no governmental body capable of governing the world. The United Nations (UN) and the various UN agencies have made good progress in improving the comparability of national aggregate data on economic and social trends (Sahlgren, 1979, 67), but the UN seems to be bogged down in attempts to improve accounting matters at the corporate level. The European Economic Community (EEC) is in the process of harmonizing standards in EEC countries. Other regional groups appear to be having varying measures of success. The voluntary world organizations such as the International Federation of Accountants (IFAC) and the International Accounting Standards Committee (IASC) may offer the best, most practical path to international harmony.

A number of regional organizations have been formed to further the interests of accounting primarily within their respective regions. These include: African Accounting Council, Southeast Asian Nations Federation of Accountants, Confederation of Asia and Pacific Accountants, Union Europenne des Expertes Comptables Economiques et Financiers, Nordic Federation of Accountants, and Associacion Interamerican de Contabilidad (Arpan and Radebaugh, 1985, 357). The countries that are members of these regional organizations are also members in the international organizations of the UN, IFAC, and IASC. Arpan and Radebaugh (1985) indicate that, "the high degree of cross-representation facilitates the process of international interaction and accounting harmonization as efforts on regional levels are quickly communicated to more global organizations, and vice versa" (360).

Some of the regional groups are formed with governmental representatives and appear to be more political in their nature: The Inter-American Accounting Association; the Conference of Asian and Pacific Accountants; the Union of European Accountants, which was replaced by the Federation des Experts Comptables Europeens in 1987 (AlHashim and Arpan, 1988, 64); and the African Accounting Council (Arpan and Radebaugh, 1985, 347). Other regional organizations are private and voluntary, for example, the Association of Accountancy Bodies in West Africa.

On a global scale, the United Nations has had a number of organizations involved in accounting standard-setting efforts since the

1970s. In 1974 in response to increasing activities of transnational corporations, the UN secretary general appointed the Group of Eminent Persons to study the impact of such corporations on development and international relations. This group "concluded that there was a need for transnational corporation reports that were comparable regardless of national origin" (Sahlgren, 1979, 67). Such reports should include "necessary economic and social information in a form that could be used by governments and other interested parties (including the international community as a whole) in evaluating the performance of transnational corporations in various areas" (67).

As a result, the UN Intergovernmental Working Group of Experts on International Standards of Accounting and Reporting, a UN commission operating under the UN Centre on Transnational Corporations, developed minimum disclosures including social responsibility matters, labor relations policies, employment breakdowns, environmental effects, and transfer pricing policy disclosures that should be made by transnational corporations to national governments. Clearly this list of subjects contains items that are well beyond the usual scope of accountants. W. John Brennan suggests that "accountants must evaluate whether such rule making is appropriately within the purvey of accountants, internationally but also nationally" (1979, 76).

Some observers believe that the UN efforts are directed largely at protecting developing nations from transnational corporations (Evans, Taylor, and Holzmann, 1985, 104). Those authors observe that because the UN does not have legal authority over transnational corporations, "each of which is safely domiciled in some country, the UN cannot require disclosure. Instead, it has tried to influence nations to require additional disclosure and to influence world public opinion along the same lines. But these tactics have not been successful thus far" (104–5).

Arpan and Radebaugh (1985) describe the UN efforts in similar tones. "In their deliberations about what the UN should do (if anything) regarding accounting standards, the ad hoc group divided sharply, largely along geographic and economic development lines. The Western industrial group did not believe the UN was the appropriate organization to set standards" (348). This group therefore, "sought to reduce the scope of proposed standards, and sought to make the form of recommendation be only illustrative of 'best practice' rather than be made mandatory. The other group, composed essentially of developing nations . . . wanted the standards to be wide ranging and mandatory" (348). As a result, "the UN's efforts have become polarized along north-south, developed-less developed political lines, with little chance for reconciliation or agreement" (348).

Several committees of OECD dealt with the transnational corporation matters of concern to the UN. The Committee on International Investment and Multinational Enterprises, apparently prodded by the UN efforts, adopted in 1976 a Declaration on International Investment and Multinational Enterprises, a code of conduct that included policies on information disclosure in annual reports and guidelines for a number of social responsibilities. OECD committees have also dealt with disclosure recommendations for security offerings and policies for transfer pricing (Evans, Taylor, and Holzmann, 1985, 105). In general, the OECD has taken positions that have already been established by its member countries and appears not to have broken new ground in regard to disclosure.

Concerns about transnational corporations that operate in developing countries are ongoing as reflected in IASC agenda-setting proposals by David Cairns, IASC secretary general (1990). In describing an IASC "comprehensive review of the financial reporting needs of developing and newly industrialized countries" (82) started in 1990, he noted that the IASC may consider whether two types of reporting might be applicable, one for domestic enterprises and the second for transnationals operating in developing countries. The second is, "the primary reason for the existence of the UN Intergovernmental Working Group of Experts on International Standards of Accounting and Reporting" (84). Cairns notes that the UN group favors more disclosures such as segment information and related party transactions, whereas both domestic enterprises in developing and developed countries are less favorably disposed. Further, he notes, "the UN Group is showing an increasing interest in disclosures that fall outside the financial statements — for example, at its meeting this month, the Group will consider disclosures relating to environmental matters" (84).

A regional governmental body playing an increasing role in international standards is the European Economic Community (EEC). The EEC is advancing toward economic integration in phases. National import tariffs and restrictions were essentially abolished in the 1960s. Economic union by the harmonization of national social, fiscal, and monetary policies is now in progress. The final goal is political union (Evans, Taylor, and Holzman, 1985, 97–98). Integrating accounting, auditing, and reporting standards within the EEC will be essential for success.

Reflecting differences in their social, legal, cultural, and economic attributes, European nations have had separate and often distinctly different standards. The divergence of EEC accounting systems is reflected in the range of groups in which EEC countries were classified in the several accounting principles models discussed above. The German and French, for example, rely on a legalistic approach. The UK follows a true and fair view that finds its basis in economic rather than legal concepts.

Harmonization of the separate country standards is being attempted by means of EEC directives. After lengthy procedures including consultation with the EEC Accounting Study Group composed of representatives from leading accounting groups in EEC countries, directives must be approved by the EEC council of ministers in cooperation with the European parliament (Van Hulle, 1989). EEC member countries are given several years to make national laws agree with the provisions of approved directives. Noncompliance can eventually lead to condemnation by the European Court of Justice.[11]

The directives are not themselves laws but are "instructions to member states to alter, if necessary, their own national legislation" (Wilson, 1991, 81). In most directive provisions, only minimum requirements are laid out. A member state may have more exacting supplementary requirements so long as they are compatible with directive provisions (81). There is considerable latitude allowed in the selection of options. The directives have improved harmonization within the EEC. But because of the many options available, harmonization has not been advanced as much as would be needed to insure reporting of similar levels of information and disclosure by all EEC companies participating in the same capital markets (81).

Christopher Nobes (1990), for example, details a number of available options in the seventh directive in which he observed "51 obvious options" (85). He concludes, "No more EC Directives on accounting are planned, so the differences discussed here will remain in 1992, and probably in 2002. Thus there is still scope for confusion and still a need for care and expertise when making European accounting comparisons" (85).

The EEC directives have been viewed by some as a hindrance to global harmonization in certain of their aspects. David Cairns, IASC secretary general, (1990) states that "the directives are a 'serious problem' and seemed to have been 'cast in stone in 1978'." He cites the valuation of financial instruments as a case in point. EC directives call for the lower of cost or market value while globally there is a movement toward marking to market value. Another problem area is goodwill that in the U.K. is written off to reserves at acquisition. The IASC intends to revise the IAS on goodwill to require capitalization and write-off against earnings over a maximum period of years (12). Fortunately, the European Commission has joined the IASC Consultative Group and indicates that it intends "to support the IASC as the appropriate channel through which to promote harmonization within the Community, and between it and outside countries" (Carey, 1990, 92).

Thus, it may be that the IASC and its companion organization, the IFAC, will be at the forefront in efforts to improve global accounting, reporting, and auditing standards. The IASC was formed in 1973 with 9 national accounting bodies as members. By 1985, membership had grown to 89 organizations representing 60 countries (Horner, 1986). Formulation of worldwide accounting standards to be observed in the presentation of financial statements is a major IASC goal. Two other important IASC objectives are to develop "a basis for underdeveloped countries to follow as an accounting profession emerged in those countries" and to increase the "focus on accounting and reporting responsibilities of multinational companies" (Wyatt, 1989, 106). The organization seeks to gain worldwide voluntary acceptance of its standards since, unlike the EEC, it does not have governmental powers.

By June 1991, there were 29 operative *international accounting standards* (IASs) (*Journal of Accountancy*, 1991). The standards have been written with harmonization rather than standardization in mind. This has caused some amount of criticism and suggested improvements. Arthur Wyatt, for example, points out that IASC standards have been written in broad terms frequently including two or more acceptable alternatives. "The standards simply were not definitive or detailed enough to cause problems in application in practice in the U.S., given the level of detail and specificity we have become accustomed to in our standards." For these reasons, the standards have been little more than a curiosity (1989, 105).

The *Journal of Accountancy* (1990) reported that in a Touche Ross International survey of 278 major multinational companies from 12 countries, two-thirds of the companies indicated that they comply substantially with IASC standards. The study was undertaken to determine the companies' views on proposals to reduce the number of alternative accounting treatments allowed under IASs. Many of the companies responded that reduction of alternatives "would improve the quality of information in published accounts of foreign companies and make the data easier to use" (15). A potential benefit of significance "was thought to be the possibility that the stock exchanges around the world would accept one set of accounts complying with IASs, instead of each requiring a new set of accounts drawn up in accordance with local accounting standards" (16).

The authority of the IASC to set international accounting standards is recognized and supported by its companion organization, The International Federation of Accountants (IFAC), which seeks "to develop and enhance a coordinated worldwide accountancy profession with harmonised standards" (Chandler, 1990). The IFAC was organized in 1977 as a global, private, voluntary organization beginning with 63 leading accounting bodies from 49 countries. IFAC membership in 1988 expanded to 105 accountancy bodies from 79 countries (1990, 84). The IFAC organizations have some one million member accountants (1989, 43).

IFAC goals include the formulation of international guidelines for auditing practices and related services. The International Auditing Practices Committee (IAPC), a standing committee formed to carry out these objectives, issued its first auditing guideline in 1980 covering the objective and scope of outside audits. As of 1990, 27 international auditing guidelines and two guidelines on related services have been issued (Chandler, 1990, 84).

The IAPC is coordinating their efforts with the International Organization of Securities Commissions and Similar Agencies (IOSCO), an organization of national securities commissions, to obtain recognition of the international auditing guidelines "for the purpose of multinational offerings of securities" (Chandler, 1989, 44). Roy Chandler (1990, 86), in discussing this development, sees that "the advantage for the securities commissions which are members of IOSCO will be a guarantee of the adequacy of standards governing the audit of financial statements involved in multinational filings, and it will remove the need for the commissions themselves to set applicable auditing standards."

Currently IAPC and IASC pronouncements are designed for harmonization and voluntary compliance. Perhaps tomorrow such global standards will become compulsory. Ed Coulson, chief accountant of the U. S. Securities and Exchange Commission, looking to the future sees a scenario in which IASC standards could evolve into a high enough set of standards that could be increasingly useful. "Eventually, the markets of the world might decide it's not worth paying for a whole bunch of individual standard setters like the FASB and the CICA and may start to use these as GAAP" (Coulson, 1989, 36).

NOTES

1. See, for example, Thomas G. Evans, Martin E. Taylor, and Oscar Holzmann (1985, 24–42); Jeffrey S. Arpan and Lee H. Radebaugh (1985, 335–44); Leslie G. Campbell (1985, 33–132); and Dhia D. AlHashim and Jeffrey S. Arpan (1988, 19–42).

2. See, for example, Gerhard G. Mueller (1967 and 1968); R. C. DaCosta, J. C. Bourgeois, and W. M. Lawson (1978); Werner G. Frank (1979), R. D. Nair, and Werner G. Frank (1980); Ahmed Belkaoui (1985); Christopher W. Nobes (1987); Gerhard Mueller, Helen Gernon, and Gary Meek (1991).

3. Those included were Austria, Belgium, Bolivia, France, Greece, Italy, Luxembourg, Paraguay, Portugal, Sweden, and Uruguay.

4. Included were Brazil, Columbia, Ethiopia, Kenya, Malaysia, Pakistan, and Singapore.

5. Included were Argentina, Australia, Bermuda, Canada, Denmark, India, Ireland, Jamaica, Mexico, Netherlands, New Zealand, Peru, Philippines, Rhodesia, South Africa, the United Kingdom, and Venezuela.

6. Jurisdictions involved included Australia, Canada, Colombia, Denmark, Germany, Hong Kong, India, Israel, Jamaica, Kenya, Netherlands, New Zealand, Pakistan, Peru, Philippines, Rhodesia, Singapore, South Africa, and the United Kingdom.

7. The eight were Argentina, Brazil, Greece, Japan, Mexico, Norway, Sweden, and Venezuela.

8. Included were Belgium, Chile, France, Guatemala, Honduras, Italy, Lebanon, Spain and Switzerland.

9. Included were the Bahamas, Bolivia, Cayman Islands, Indonesia, Netherlands Antilles, Nicaragua, Panama, Paraguay, and Uruguay.

10. Included were the Bahamas, Cayman Islands, Indonesia, Netherlands, Antilles, Paraguay, and Uruguay.

11. See Richard Vangermeersch (1985) for an informative report on the procedures for approving an EEC directive.

3

Accounting Impacts from a Corporate Context

Companies operating across national borders must deal with complex accounting problems not found in domestic operations. The types of international accounting problems encountered depend in part upon the operations being carried out. Problems of an accounting nature are fewer when products or services are bought or sold across borders without direct cross-border investment. Entities that make direct foreign investment, however, must master a variety of problems that are inherent in such activities.

The multinational corporation (MNC) with operations in many countries must cope with differing languages, currencies, accounting standards, laws, and customs. Corporate accounting and reporting on a global basis is required. Yet, reporting must be structured for decision making both at headquarters and at local units. Planning and control functions, including the transfer pricing of goods and services, must adapt to greater diversity. Performance evaluation must take into consideration a wide variety of differing local environmental factors. Information and communication systems on a global scale must be used. Such expanded, diverse operations and systems need expanded internal control, audit, and management accounting.

Reporting, especially to interests outside the corporation, is often required on a global basis, requiring accounting consolidations with attendant complexities. The requirement for consolidated statements, while not universally recognized in many countries, is growing in acceptance as the proper approach to reporting for MNCs that are, after all, under control of one unified management and operate as one economic whole regardless of the myriad legal forms that may be taken. By aggregating parent and subsidiaries into one set of financial statements, reporting and decision making for the entire economic entity is enhanced. Yet, in consolidated reports, important details about geographical regions, product lines, or other major segments of the total business are obscured or hidden. Segmental reporting must accompany consolidation to disaggregate important information for decision making.

Accounting in each local jurisdiction must be adequate for local uses. For consolidation purposes, global accounting records must be transformed to a common basis. The basis may be that of the country in which the MNC is headquartered or it may be that of the country in which capital or credit is obtained. Accounts from different countries, which will typically have different inflation rates, are usually kept in local language and in local currency. These accounts require translation into one language, one reporting currency. If local accounting standards are used, adjustments are required to make all reports consistent with the home country or the reporting country accounting standards.

Some MNCs produce financial reports using several national bases. The extent to which MNCs prepare differing financial statements for external use and make adequate disclosures appears often to depend upon where they raise capital. If most capital is raised in the home country, little benefit comes from offering differing external financial statements. However, when capital is raised in many jurisdictions, disclosures of all types are likely to increase. It has been reported that disclosure levels are significantly increased when new sources of investment funds are sought (Mueller, Gernon, and Meek, 1991, 65). Further, studies have concluded "that differences in disclosure levels among nations are rapidly narrowing, and that increased disclosure can lead to lower costs of capital for business enterprises" (65).

Financial statements and disclosures may come in a variety of forms. Some MNCs may have their financial statements translated into other languages but still retain home country currency and standards. Others may convert their financial reports by adjusting currency and standards to the currency and standards of the foreign user's country. This restatement may be in total or on a partial basis. Increasingly MNCs are preparing financial statements using International Committee on Accounting Standards (IASC) standards. Mueller, Gernon, and Meek believe that "no matter what local reporting requirements dictate, a multinational company is at some disadvantage unless it follows 'world class' financial reporting" (1991, 5). Financial analysis of reports and statements, however prepared, should take into consideration the differing financial and business practices under which operations took place, since substantially different customs and business norms are found in various countries.

Changing prices create difficulties in domestic accounting when high inflation makes historical, cost-based accounting systems less reliable in purchasing power terms. Accounting across national borders has the added problem of changing currency conversion rates between countries, which of course are caused in some measure by differing domestic inflation rates in the countries involved.

Information on general price level or specific price level changes have generally not been incorporated into primary external financial statements, although there have been a number of exceptions, particularly in Dutch financial reports and in countries that have experienced persistently high inflation. In the introduction to IAS No. 15, the IASC noted, "In most countries, such information is supplementary to, but not a part of, the primary financial statements" (IASC, 1981, 11, 245). The committee concluded that there is not as yet a consensus on the subject and suggested that supplementary disclosures to the primary financial statements on the historical, cost basis would assist the evolution of reporting the effects of price changes.

As high inflation rates became persistent in the late 1970s in the United States, mandatory supplementary information of selected items on a current cost and constant dollar basis was required in the United States by *Statement of Financial Accounting Standards (SFAS) No. 33* (U.S. Financial Accounting Standards Board [hereafter, FASB], 1979). After a five-year experimental period the supplemental reporting was made voluntary. In the U.K. the Accounting Standards Committee's *Statement of Standard Accounting Practice No. 16*, "Current Cost Accounting" (1980) was issued on a three-year experimental basis. The standard allowed firms to present current cost information as either supplementary or primary so long as adequate historical, cost information was also provided. Mandatory provisions of the U.K. standard were suspended in May 1985.

After reviewing the history of inflation and current cost accounting, Dhia D. AlHashim and Jeffrey S. Arpan noted that countries have made a number of attempts to deal with inflation in accounting reports as high inflation rates tended to be persistent. "However, whenever inflation somewhat subsides, these countries typically revert to the historical cost standard, which has been prevalent throughout the entire existence of financial accounting" (1988, 109).

The fundamental problem with price level accounting appears to be the lack of objective evidence of either general or specific price change measurement. Historical cost, based in completed market transactions, provides a more objective measure for recording corporate financial history. In some countries that have experienced hyperinflation, valuation adjustments are directed by the government. Brazil and Chile are two examples (AlHashim and Arpan, 1988, 116–18). This provides a somewhat more objective, if arbitrary, basis for adjustments.

Changes in currency exchange rates, whether caused by inflation or other factors, can markedly affect results of cross-currency transactions and can markedly affect translation of cross-currency financial statements. The ways in which gains, losses, and currency translation differences are accounted for can also markedly affect the portrayal of operating results and financial position. Companies that have significant operations in other than their reporting currency must translate local currency accounting records into reporting currency equivalents if global consolidated financial statements are to be prepared. Currency translations for financial reporting purposes are called for as well when transactions denominated in other than the reporting currency remain incomplete at report date.

The need for currency translation of intracompany reports may depend upon several factors. If cross-border branches or subsidiaries need tight planning and control from home office, all reports may be needed in home office currency. Since local operations almost certainly will be conducted in local currency, a two-way translation process would be necessary. That is, planning and control reporting from the home office to a branch may be planned and controlled at headquarters in the home office currency and must be translated to local currency for local operational use. A reverse process would be needed when reports are sent from a branch to the home office. Where subsidiaries operate more independently, operations might be planned and controlled in local currency with translation into home office currency for financial reporting requirements. It seems logical that with more or less independent local operations, central managers need to be able to use budgets and reports productively in a number of local currencies.

In the matter of the importance of using local currency denominated reports for local operations, Choi and Mueller make the point that "evaluation of local competitive conditions and comparisons with similar local firms are difficult unless locally oriented accounting information is available" (1984, 110). Further, they observe, "accounting information requirements of a parent company should generally not be allowed to overshadow local accounting information requirements. In effect, two distinct sets of information requirements exist and they require translation and reconciliation back and forth" (111).

The selection of the appropriate currency exchange rate is an accounting dilemma. The exchange rate in effect at the time the market transaction took place appears consistent with historical-based costing.

However, since currency conversion rates change over time, there is the possibility of using either the current or historical rates in the assumed currency conversions when translating foreign statements to a reporting currency.

When buy or sell transactions are undertaken, foreign country currency must actually be converted to home currency. Currency exchange gain or loss becomes part of transaction results as actual currency conversion takes place. Transactions denominated in home country currency cause no related accounting problems. The party on the other end of the transaction who must convert to local currency assumes the risk of and accounts for changes in the exchange rate and the resulting gain or loss.

Should gain or loss be netted against transaction totals? Or should gain or loss be separately recorded? If separately recorded, should it be reflected in the income statement of the period or carried forward in balance sheet amounts? What should be done if financial statements are prepared after the transaction is originally recorded but before settlement? Accounting treatments differ in the various countries.

The FASB determined that transaction gain or loss should be accounted for separately. This procedure appears to be accepted in a majority of world jurisdictions. Under U.S. standards (FASB, 1975, 4), completed or not, transaction exchange gains or losses are treated as normal operating items and are reflected immediately in income. If settlement has not occurred, the exchange rate current at the statement date is used to determine unrealized gain or loss. In many other national jurisdictions, recognition of gains and losses is deferred until the transaction is complete and cash is received or paid. Further, many country standards do not treat these gains or losses as income statement items but instead they adjust the balance sheet amounts (AlHashim and Arpan, 1988, 141).

The fundamental difference between transactions and translations should be noted. Accounting for transactions includes actual conversions from one to another currency. The risk of changing rates must be borne by one party or another to the transaction. Translation results in the expression of financial reports at a point in time in the currency of a country in which the transaction did not take place and where currency conversions did not occur. Translation is for the purpose of providing information denominated in a single, reporting currency whether or not transactions actually occurred in that currency.

Translation of accounting reports denominated in a currency other than the reporting currency can be accomplished by at least four different methods: the current rate method; the current, noncurrent method; the monetary, nonmonetary method; and the temporal method. In each, the invested equity account is always translated at the historical rate. Retained earnings is a composite of past income summaries. Each method requires a residual balancing account for the net effects of translation. Whether net translation effects should be included in the income statement or carried forward in a balance sheet account is a matter of some controversy.

Under the current rate method, all assets and liability accounts are translated to the reporting currency using the current exchange rate in effect at statement closing date. Income statement accounts are translated at the exchange rate in effect when revenues and expenses are recognized. For simplicity, this generally is done by applying an appropriately weighted average rate for the period. This is a simple and direct method that retains the relationships of account balances as they were prior to translation. Only the monetary form is changed. Consolidations over time include the current, changing conditions of the foreign currency of each foreign unit. As exchange rates change over time, the method does not preserve historical costs.

This being the case, another translation method is needed that will allow foreign unit consolidation reflective of accounting principles of the reporting corporation. Several systems have been developed that use historical or current exchange rates, whichever better reflect parent's accounting valuation bases for the particular account.

With the current-noncurrent method, the current exchange rate at the statement date is used to translate current assets and liabilities. Exchange rates in effect when the originating transactions occurred are used for noncurrent assets and liabilities. These are the so-called historical rates. In the income statement, the weighted average exchange rate for the current year is applied to all accounts except those related to balance sheet accounts that were translated using historical rates, for example, depreciation on fixed assets. The current-noncurrent method, which takes a maturity date point of reference, was widely used in the United States prior to publication of FASB publication No. 8 (1975). Current items expected to be settled within one year were converted at the current exchange rate and the related gain or loss recognized. The method assumes that the realization or payment of cash would be in the reporting currency at the current rate of exchange.

The monetary-nonmonetary method calls for translating all monetary assets and liabilities at the current exchange rate while nonmonetary balance sheet accounts are translated at historical exchange rates at transaction dates. As in the other methods, contributed equity is translated at the historical rate and retained earnings are a composite taken from successive income translations. Rather than basing assumed conversion on maturity date, this method moves toward consideration of the nature of the valuation basis of each account. By their nature monetary accounts are fixed in a particular monetary unit. As conversion rates change, valuation of monetary accounts should change with resulting recognition of unrealized currency conversion gains or losses.

The temporal method uses neither current-noncurrent nor monetary-nonmonetary classification to decide translation rates. Rather, the translation rate appropriate to the measurement nature of each account prior to translation is used. The currency conversion process should change only the unit of measure, not the valuation basis of each item. The temporal method allows translation consistent with the valuation basis of the reporting entity, whether that be historical cost, replacement, or current cost based. For cash, receivables, and payables, which are monetary in nature and are carried at amounts currently owned or expected to be received or paid in the future, the current exchange rate is used. For accounts carried at original cost, the historical exchange rate in effect at the time of the original market transaction is used. The account valuation basis used prior to translation is thus maintained, only the monetary unit is changed. The method appears to allow translations more consistent with the original nature of the accounts. It has the advantage of being applicable to bases of accounting other than historical cost, such as replacement or current costs. In these cases, the current conversion rate would be used. Income statement items are translated at an average rate for the current year except for those related to balance sheet accounts translated using historical rates of exchange. Results are very similar to the monetary-nonmonetary method except that the temporal reasoning is applicable to differing valuation bases.

Predominant translation practices in 53 countries were tabulated by Choi and Mueller (1984, 161–62). The current method is employed by 25 of the countries. The current-noncurrent method is used by 7 countries. The monetary-nonmonetary method is used by 10 countries. The temporal method is used by 14 countries. Canada, the United Kingdom, and the United States are listed as having both the current and the temporal methods as predominant.

A major inherent problem in accounting for cross-border transactions is that exchange rates are subject to continuous change. The *Wall Street Journal*'s Randall Smith, highlighting the growth of currencies markets, wrote about "a market that has mushroomed so much since exchange rates were unfixed in 1973 that it now dwarfs the stock market" (1991, 1). Currency volatility can cause substantial unrealized transaction or translation gains or losses to be reported in a given year. If rates subsequently change direction, reported earnings can be affected substantially in reverse fashion. Inclusions of the unrealized currency gains or losses in income would seem to be justified if the realization is expected. But (as is the case when using market values for other accounting purposes) conversion market rates are subject to change before the transactions are actually completed. This is particularly significant for an affiliated foreign business unit that will not complete the transactions for some years.

The dilemma of "yo-yo" earnings effects has been somewhat alleviated by *SFAS No. 52* (FASB, 1981) that takes the view that methods of translation should depend upon the environment in which the unit operates and in which it generates cash flows. If a particular unit functions primarily in a local currency, the current rate method is prescribed with deferral of translation gains or losses. If the functional currency is the reporting currency, in this case the U.S. dollar, then the temporal approach should still be used with attendant recognition of gains or losses in current income.

A particular foreign subsidiary may be operating in the long term in a foreign country. The subsidiary's cash flow may be in the local currency. Business may be conducted mostly in the local environment with few intercompany transactions with the parent firm. The unit may not expect to liquidate its foreign business but rather expects to be a long-term going concern in that foreign jurisdiction. It appears to make little sense to view this subsidiary as though it were doing business in other than the foreign currency. Under these circumstances, it would not appear that unrealized gain or loss from assumed conversions, necessary to translate accounts to the reporting currency, should be included in income.

SFAS No. 52 directs that the current rate method be used for all assets and liabilities of a foreign entity that, in terms of its business operations, uses a foreign currency as its functional currency, that is, the currency in which it conducts business. A weighted average exchange rate is used for the income statement. Any translation gains or losses are not reported in income but are deferred in a separate equity account that will accumulate translation adjustments until such time as the foreign subsidiary is liquidated or a change in the economic situation of the unit occurs.

If a subsidiary using the current rate method is located in a country that experiences high rates of inflation versus inflation rates in the parent's country, over a period of years the currency exchange rates would favor the parent country's currency. This will make translations using current exchange rates reflect increasingly lower amounts of fixed assets, for example, in parent's currency in consolidated reports. This would not be the case if subsidiary statements were price-level adjusted prior to translation. It would seem that lacking the price-level adjustments, which are not permitted by *SFAS No. 52*, misleading reports could be produced. The *SFAS* partially addresses the problem by requiring the temporal method for translation of units in countries that experience a rate of inflation of 100 percent or more in a three-year period. Under the temporal method, long-lived assets would be translated at historical rates of exchange.

While the translation problem and the price level problem may seem similar in nature, Choi and Mueller clearly point out the difference. "Foreign exchange translation is largely a unit-of-account (measurement unit) problem. Price level adjustment is primarily concerned with the distinction between capital and income and, therefore, has predominantly valuation (measurement process) implications" (1984, 190). Price level adjustments to external financial reports are not generally required and seem unlikely to be in the future. The decision arises in few countries of which to apply first — translation from local to reporting currency or restatement for the effects of inflation.[1]

The issues involved in the "restate-translate" or "translate-restate" problem may be more important for internal reporting. If the accounts of foreign operations can be reliably restated for price level changes, including current costs of the foreign country, then the current rate translation method that uses the closing exchange rate would appear to offer a valid reporting process. If complete current cost-constant dollar statements cannot be prepared, some subset may be appropriate for internal reporting and management use. The difficulties inherent in this process, however, are implicit in the conclusion drawn by J. M. Samuels and A. G. Piper. "The logic and potential simplicity of 'current values translated at current rates' has not found favour due to the practical problems of determining current values and the weight of tradition favouring the historical cost basis for the original financial data" (1985, 126).

Inflation does affect operations and planning both on a global basis and on a local level where managers may become preoccupied with coping with inflation to the detriment of normal activities. George M. Scott indicates the importance of the effects of changing prices on successful worldwide planning. "Differing rates of inflation mean that real costs of production and other factors change dynamically relative to one another so that a global system must be continuously cost balanced." This may result "in the shifting of production and other resources among countries as relative costs change" (1978, 1,212).

Planning and control is thus dependent upon national environments in which firms operate. Differing economic, political, and business conditions add greatly to the complexity of international planning and control tasks. Governmental regulations, laws, and taxes vary as do business practices, customs, and conditions. Scott grouped international environmental complexities that have significant impact on planning and control as "communications differences, cultural differences, environmental changes, differing price levels and the diversity of economic, political and business operating conditions encountered" (1978, 1209–10).

Planning and control often require personal interactions as well as written communications. Both are much more complicated and time-consuming when national borders are crossed. A common language may not be used. Distances can be great, necessitating larger travel and communication expenses with attendant complexities. Cross-border communication systems may be incompatible or at differing levels of expertise. Government control and intervention in communications may be encountered.[2]

Managers in various parts of the world have many of the same attitudinal problems that domestic managers have regarding budgeting and control. In addition, in some cases "managers from different cultures have culture-related attributes which reduce the effectiveness of planning and control processes" (Scott, 1978, 1210). Some may think that control processes are demeaning or unjust. The local manager's concepts of time importance may differ, causing untimely planning and control processes. Some may view the budgeting process as trivial. Managers "may have too little empathy for cultures other than their own, which can affect their relations with associates in other countries" (1211). Some may prefer more independence rather than collaboration. There may be resistance to change. Most of these problems are not unique to international operations, but planning and control is made more difficult and time-consuming as the scope of international operations and the variety of local managers with differing social and cultural attitudes become greater.

Operations planned for and carried out across national borders tend to become more complex as the number of countries increases. Environmental diversity is increased with attendant effects upon planning and control. Constraints placed on operations by the various environments differ. What is possible in one nation may be impossible or simply different in another. Environmental factors in a single nation do tend to change slowly. Yet, national rates of change differ. "The result is greater dynamism of the total environment of international companies; controls and plans implemented today may be appropriate now but obsolete

tomorrow, next week, or next month when the environments change relative to each other" (Scott, 1978, 1211).

While planning, control, and evaluation have, of course, been carried out for many years by corporations, Mueller, Gernon, and Meek believe that "the development of comprehensive MNC international planning and control systems with long-range strategic focus is new" (1991, 104). The MNC needs to include each foreign operating location in its global strategic planning. This is a higher order of complexity from domestic-only environments because it entails the economic, social, legal, and political characteristics in each foreign location. Mueller, Gernon, and Meek suggest six phases that the MNC management control system should address: assessment of relevant environmental variables, assessment relative to its own environment of each subsidiary's strengths and weaknesses, setting objectives and priorities, developing budgets and standards of operations for performance assessment, measuring output, and providing feedback through evaluations (105).

Differences in planning, controlling, and evaluating between domestic and foreign operations do seem in large measure to gear on the complexities of differing environmental factors. In turn, these appear to create obstacles to global uniform corporate reporting "and simply requiring uniformity does not make these barriers disappear" (Mueller, Gernon, and Meek, 1991, 108).

In Third World countries, for example, adequate accounting may not be widespread or in some cases even available. Yet, the MNC, if it is to compare reports and evaluations of all its subsidiaries', needs consistent and comparable accounting and reports. In pursuit of this goal, Mueller, Gernon, and Meek believe that MNCs should require reporting by subsidiaries using the parent's home country standards. At the same time, they recognize that the accounting and reporting systems must "remain adaptive and flexible to the information needs of both corporate head-quarters and the operating subsidiaries. Nevertheless, adaptability is an obstacle to uniformity, and vice versa" (108).

Planning and control for a given company can be carried out in many forms. Two apparently polar styles of control, which have been discussed by many authors, are related to the degree of control by the parent company and the international integration of operations. Scott (1978, 1213) for example refers to the corporation as the multinational holding company (MHC) and the multinational enterprise (ME), which is referred to by others as the MNC. ME and MNC are used interchangeably in this book.

The MHC's foreign subsidiaries manufacture and sell products within a single foreign country with little interaction between either other foreign jurisdictions or the parent. Products and operations are likely to be similar in nature to those carried out by the MHC in its home country. Subsidiaries in each foreign country are likely to have local autonomy for operations, which may be viewed as investment centers for accounting and evaluation purposes. Interchanges with parents are limited largely to investment funds to a subsidiary from the MHC and returns of profits in various forms to the MHC.

The MNC, however, is viewed as being globally coordinated toward the goal of maximizing global returns on investments. Companies are thought to move from the MHC through various stages of global coordination in which operations in all countries tend to become "integrated vertically and horizontally and coordinated on a worldwide basis to the extent that this is possible within the constraints imposed by national governments' policies and the limitations of managerial and information systems technology" (Scott, 1978, 1214).

The global coordination style of management and control causes a dilemma of centralized versus decentralized control that is similar to domestic operations but appears to be more complex in international spheres. Managers of local operations are in the better position to understand and respond to changing local conditions. Headquarter managers are in the better position to understand and to make decisions on a global basis in the best interests of the company as a whole. The planning and control systems of the MNC need to allow for the pooling and integration of both aspects. This dilemma of centralized versus decentralized planning and control is, of course, present in domestic corporations. The process becomes more complex on an international basis, yet an adequate solution is more important because of the geographical spread, the complexity, and the large size of operations.

Scott suggests that flexible and adaptable, coordinated management is needed that will integrate the levels of management in good planning so that each can provide needed information and perspectives. "A great deal of corporate inculcation, teamwork and mutual reliance, and joint decision making is required to make this system effective" (1978, 1215). Local managers are more likely to have the better view of and information about functions such as manufacturing, marketing, and local finances. Headquarters is more likely to have better information and views on global marketplaces.

Long-range planning and capital budgeting in the MHC tend to center on the local host country. The corporate plan aggregates planning for individual host country operations. The MNC it would appear needs to have "simultaneous participation in long-term planning by both head-quarters and local entity planners" (Scott, 1228). Local conditions on costs and other markets that can best be provided by local managers are needed so that global alternatives can be evaluated.

Companies that are better able to move toward global integration would seem to have substantial competitive advantages in the global market-place. National governments often restrict functions critical to the ME, thereby restricting or making more difficult global coordination and maxi-mization. However difficult and complex, global planning and control functions appear needed to allow rapid, flexible adaptation to changing local and global conditions. "Indeed, the company that simply utilizes its domestic control systems abroad, as many U.S. companies have been wont to do, will experience grave control problems in its international systems, and will find itself unable to operate as a coordinated ME" (Scott, 1978, 1221).

Whatever the planning and control system used, performance evalua-tions both in domestic and international spheres, it is generally agreed, should separate evaluation of the unit from evaluation of the manager. Some factors that greatly affect the performance of the unit may not be under control or influence of the manager. The information system in use must be able to collect needed information for both types of evaluations. The purposes of global evaluation systems according to Alan C. Shapiro (1978, 454) are to provide for rational global resource allocations, to pro-vide early warning if current operations go wrong, to evaluate individual manager performance, and to have a set of standards that will motivate managers.

Profit and investment centers would appear to be useful for all of these purposes for the MHC. Such centers appear to be more useful for the first two than the latter two purposes. Local MHC managers are in control of most aspects of their operations and can be held responsible accordingly. Performance evaluation systems based on profit or investment centers do appear appropriate for the MNC unit but appear less appropriate for the evaluation of local managers since many functions in the MNC unit are not under local manager control.

Budgets offer another practical, although possibly less effective, approach to the evaluation of managers and units of both MHCs and MNCs. It would seem that the profit plan should be constructed in a participative manner between different management levels. Budget variances for aspects that are under local control can then be the basis for performance evaluations. Many important nonfinancial factors can also provide the basis for evaluations between expected and actual performance.

Scott notes that profit centers, while criticized for theoretical short-comings, are widely and successfully used in domestic operations. He believes that profit centers are less useful for both MNHs and MNCs for a number of reasons including the lack of uniform environment, the lack of an in-depth understanding of the foreign environment by headquarters, differing inflation rates, and "severe transfer pricing problems encountered in international operations" (1978, 1232).

Wagdy M. Abdallah (1984) surveyed 64 MNCs and found that respondents indicated some differences between performance evaluation measures for managers and for their units. Profit measures were used by 78 percent of respondents for subsidiary performance evaluations but only 66 percent for manager performance. Return on investment was used by 74 percent for subsidiary performance but by 67 percent for manager performance. Respondents' use of budget controls appeared to be about even. Budget compared to actual profit was used by 87 percent for managers and 86 percent for subsidiaries. Budget compared to actual return on investment was used by 64 percent for managers and 66 percent for subsidiaries.

A major obstacle to treating foreign units as profit or investment centers appears to be the ways in which transfer prices are used by MNCs. Transfer prices between domestic units tend to be set on an equitable basis. In international operations, transfer prices appear to be set with other objectives in mind. This is anything but a trivial matter as indicated by Choi and Mueller. "It is estimated that about 40 percent of all international trade consists of transfers between related business entities" (1984, 433). As international business expands, transfer pricing becomes ever more important.

There are a number of corporate goals that can be served by transfer pricing. Profit center motivation and accountability has traditionally been the central issue for domestic units. Internationally, transfer pricing policies can be useful to avoid tax in some jurisdictions and to transfer cash from one country to another. Such use can, of course, be in conflict with goals of governments.

Mueller, Gernon, and Meek enumerate the objectives that, although unnecessary for domestic operations, international transfer pricing policies must attempt to accomplish: minimization of worldwide income taxes and import duties, avoidance of financial restrictions, managing currency fluctuations, and winning host country approval (1991, 128).

A study by Jane O. Burns (1980) responded to by senior financial officers of 62 U.S. multinational companies disclosed that the U.S. managers of 97 percent of the firms controlled global intracompany pricing decisions. The survey asked respondents to indicate the importance of 14 factors in making transfer pricing decisions. Responses indicated that decisions were "substantially influenced by several external pressures" (38). The top five rated factors were competition in the foreign country, market conditions in the foreign country, reasonable profit for foreign affiliates, U.S. federal income taxes, and taxation in the foreign country. These were followed, in rank order, by economic conditions in the foreign country, import restrictions, price controls, exchange controls, customs duties, U.S. export incentives, management of cash flows, floating exchange rates, and other U.S. federal taxes.

A study by Seung H. Kim and Stephen W. Miller, "Constituents of the International Transfer Pricing Decision," reported in the *Columbia Journal of World Business*, Spring 1979, was discussed by Choi and Mueller (1984, 443–44). This survey concentrated on U.S.–based MNCs with affiliates in developing countries as opposed to the highly industrialized countries used in the Burns' study. Kim and Miller found that the environmental influences in the developing countries on transfer prices were in rank order: profit repatriation restrictions within the host country, exchange controls, joint-venture constraints within the host country, tariffs and customs duties within the host country, income tax liability within the host country, income tax liability within the United States, quota restrictions within the United States, credit status of the U.S. parent firm, and credit status of foreign affiliates. As in the Burns' study, the list of variables was limited by the factors that Kim and Miller selected to study.

Choi and Mueller suggest that "whereas earlier studies identified income tax liabilities as highly influential factors in transfer pricing decisions in general, current research suggests that the influence of a given variable will vary with the nature of a particular foreign environment" (1984, 444). This may be reflective of "an emerging consensus among host governments that arm's length pricing is the appropriate norm in arriving at profits for tax purposes" (439).

A complex system of pricing between corporate or controlled units can require substantial costs and managerial time that might be used in other pursuits. "Yet despite these problems and an inherent desire to keep things simple," Christopher Nobes and Robert Parker observed "the advantages of transfer price manipulation remain considerable, given the market imperfections of today's international business environment" (1988, 175).

Intracorporate transfers lack the valuation basis of arm's-length transactions and must be priced in some other manner. No one pricing system seems able to fit all needs. Cost or market-based pricing systems have well-known advantages and disadvantages.

An important attribute of transfer pricing is that the transfer takes place within one company. The controlling interest managers are relatively free to set transfer prices as they wish within governmental restrictions. They can be expected to attempt to maximize total global corporate value in which two aspects seem important to consider — earnings with related taxation and cash flow. If the transfer price is set higher than an arm's-length price, earnings and cash flow are increased to the transferring unit from the receiving unit. Set transfer price lower than the arm's-length price and the reverse effects occur.

Transfer pricing of this nature may be a tool, for example, where tax rates are unequal, where there are restrictions on cash flows, where there are price controls on goods, where import duties are not larger than tax rates, where the exchange rate is unstable, and where political or other pressures make transfers advisable (Lall, 1973, 412). To use transfer pricing policies to attain the global goals of maximizing profits and reducing risks appears to be a complex undertaking. The volume of intracorporate trade is much larger than the flow of dividends and other means of investment return between parent and units in other jurisdictions. Transfer pricing therefore appears to offer opportunities that corporations may find difficult to resist. To the extent that transfer prices do not reflect arm's-length prices, economic efficiency may be impaired.

Transfer pricing practices can have severe effects upon less-developed countries. Sanjaya Lall (1973) concludes that "the cards are in fact stacked heavily against the less-developed economies" (416). In such countries, tax rates are often higher. Import duties on manufacturing inputs are relatively low. Balance-of-payments are often a problem with restrictions in force. The political and governmental environment in less developed countries "also tends to be inimical to the free operation and expansion of MNEs" (416). Lall suggests that this creates a dilemma for less developed countries in that they must conform to "norms of the developed world" (416) to avoid having transfer pricing policies used against them.

Transfer pricing policies set for alternative goals do seem to be in conflict with the traditional goals of profit center motivation and accountability. As to this aspect, Lall observes, "all that is required is that the MNE keep two sets of accounts, one showing 'real' profits and the other taxable profits; keeping two account books is one of the oldest business practices in the world and certainly not beyond the capacity of MNEs" (1973, 418).

Since 1976, a complicating factor for U.S. multinationals arises from *SFAS No. 14*, "Financial Reporting for Segments of a Business Enterprise," that requires segment information to include intraenterprise sales or transfers between geographic areas to be accounted for on the basis used by the enterprise to price the intraenterprise sales or transfers. The basis of accounting for intraenterprise transfers or sales must also be disclosed (FASB, 1976, 18).

Whether treated as a profit center or as a budget controlled unit, the amount of required data and communications in the planning and control process depends in part on the independence of local managers and the coordinating management systems used. Ongoing developments in communications systems are greatly aiding these processes. Computers are now linked across the globe in on-line, real-time systems. Mail communications have taken on electronic forms via telephone linked facsimile transmission machines. Electronic mail via computer transmission lines is now instantaneous. Although communications across great distances are not perfect, problems are diminishing.

Accounting information systems must provide for local and consolidated external and internal reporting. External reporting in an accounting context generally takes the form of annual financial statements, tax returns, and other required government reports that must be prepared according to the needs and requirements of various external users.

Internal reporting is frequently based on accounting procedures and practices required for external reporting. Many internal variations are, of course, in use that enhance information for decision making. Direct costing is used, for example, in place of full absorption costing. Responsibility accounting procedures report both variable and fixed costs separately and controllable and uncontrollable costs separately. The internal reports are generally reconcilable with external reports. These functions are true in domestic as well as international accounting systems.

Just as for a domestic corporation, the accounting information system for an international company must be compatible with the organizational form adopted. Mueller, Gernon, and Meek (1991) suggest that MNC organizational form and control depend upon the parent's management attitudes. These authors approach international corporate structure and control in a manner somewhat different than Mueller et al. (1991) as ethnocentric, polycentric, and geocentric. An ethnocentric approach is home country oriented in which home country procedures are used worldwide. The polycentric approach is host country oriented and allows local autonomy. The geocentric approach focuses on the world as a whole and requires evaluation and control systems that are both local and global (1991, 95–97).

Four common forms of MNC organization are: grouping by the international division in which all foreign operations are organized separately from domestic divisions, grouping by product line, grouping by geographical areas, and grouping by the global matrix organization, which is a blend of more than one of the other methods (Mueller et al., 1991, 93–94).

The accounting information system must be compatible with the organizational structure and designed to supply requisite information to appropriate levels of decision making. The larger the MNC, the more complex will be the accounting system. The degree of centralization or decentralization is important to determining decision-making points and the information needs of each. As observed by Scott earlier, Mueller, Gernon, and Meek state, "For years U.S. companies have used basically the same accounting information system to collect and process data from foreign and domestic operations" (1991, 98). This policy was less expensive and easier since management was familiar with existing systems. "However, exported versions of the domestic control system are seldom as successful or effective internationally as they are domestically" (98). Domestic systems are made to be consistent with home country environment factors. "Exporting such a system ignores the foreign subsidiary's operating environment and may result in a breakdown of communication" (98).

Whatever systems are used, the magnitude of the additional complexities in communicating with and managing of global organizations is great. Dhia D. AlHashim and Jeffrey S. Arpan's apt description seems appropriate. "For large MNEs, the amount of information is staggering. Hence, MNEs use incredible international information systems to collect, store, and direct information to the right people at the right time. The process of monitoring and evaluating what actually occurs in the firm's operations is awesome" (1988, 173).

The scale, geographical spread, and diversity of additional accounting systems and problems that must be handled by an international company requires auditing on a global scale. The effects on public accounting firms are discussed in other parts of this book. The effects upon internal auditing, while not as far reaching, are nevertheless substantial.

As an indication of the increasing global scope of internal audit, The Institute of Internal Auditors (IIA) founded in 1941 grew to 200 chapters by 1991, with worldwide membership in excess of 43,000 internal auditors in more than 100 countries. In addition to the United States, national IIA institutes operate in Australia, the People's Republic of China, France, India, Israel, Italy, Japan, Malaysia, Mexico, New Zealand, the Philippines, South Africa, and the United Kingdom.

Requirements for and use of corporate internal audit in countries varies from little to heavy use. Surprisingly, the U.K. and Japan seem to make much less use of internal audit than one might expect. A survey conducted by Aid to Industry Ltd. and the Institute of Internal Auditors-U.K. found that of 1,200 British firms responding, only 24 percent had an internal audit function (*Internal Auditor*, 1991, 11). And, from their study of Japanese corporations, Arthur R. Kagle, Takamike Fujimoto, and Seiichiro Shimogaki report that "there appears to be almost a consensus among Japanese managers that the need for audit, especially internal audit within the Japanese firm, is less than it is for Western companies" (Kagle, Fujimoto, and Shimogaki, 1988, 51).

U.S. MNCs must have substantial resources devoted to internal controls and internal audit if for no other reason than to comply with the Foreign Corrupt Practices Act (Public Law 95–213) passed in 1977, which requires that accounting records be accurately and fairly kept in sufficient detail to disclose transactions and the disposition of assets. A formal internal audit function is required. A system of internal control must be maintained that is sufficient to provide reasonable assurance that transactions are executed according to management's authorizations, to allow financial statements in accordance with generally accepted accounting principles and other criteria applicable, and to maintain accountability over assets. Such records must be reconciled with assets at reasonable intervals. The act was directed at discouraging bribery. Its provisions go well beyond any previous legislation in requiring proper records with adequate internal control. Civil and criminal penalties can apply for firms and executives for noncompliance.

Canada passed The Canadian Financial Administration Act in 1984 with similar internal audit and broader external audit requirements. The Canadian act "provides that internal audits are to be carried out to assess compliance with the responsibilities of management" (Radburn, 1986, 20) regarding safeguarding and control of assets, compliance with the act and other regulations, and "systems and practices that provide both for the economic and efficient management of resources and the effectiveness of operations" (20).

External audit was expanded by the act requiring not only the annual audit of financial statements but a comprehensive audit at least every five years by an examiner, normally the external auditor, who is to determine whether "the various management control systems, financial control systems, management information systems and management practices of the corporation were maintained" to assure that assets were safeguarded and controlled, corporate resources (financial, human, and physical) were "managed economically and efficiently," (21) and operations were carried out effectively. These requirements for internal control and internal audit appear to be among the most rigorous in the world.

The need for increased internal audit is paralleled by the magnitude of changes that the growth of international business has had on corporate accounting. In the words of William E. Langdon, executive vice-president of The Society of Management Accountants of Canada, "International business is turning management accounting into a global profession, unrestricted by national boundaries" (1986, 58). That this is so can be seen in the many corporate accounting issues already discussed. It is not surprising that Langdon estimates that "management accounting is practiced by about 60% of the world's professional accountants" (58).

NOTES

1. For several articles on these issues, see S. J. Gray (Ed.) (1983) *International Accounting and Transnational Decisions*, London: Butterworth.

2. See Joseph L. Sardinas, Jr. and Susan Merrill (1987, 305–15) for a discussion of the regulatory environment of cross-border data communications and an analysis of possible problems.

II

SOME ECONOMIC
CONSIDERATIONS

4

International Business Services in a Developmental Context

The second half of the twentieth century has been characterized by the ascendancy of service activities to prominence in various economies throughout the world. To some extent service ascendancy has been seen by economists as paralleling economic growth. Writing in 1988, Leslie Castle and Christopher Findley pointed to three hypotheses supporting that contention. "The first stresses differential effects of income growth on the demand for services relative to the demand for manufactures including agricultural products" (4).

The second hypothesis cited has to do with the presumption that service pursuits are lower in productivity than are various other activities. Of course that perception has been around for some time and seems to suggest that the impressive expansion in service employment may be the seat of inefficiency or forms of disguised unemployment. Without reviewing comparisons of the general productivity of services as compared to manufacturing, in the present context it should be sufficient to point to the size and diversity of the service sector and hence to the futility of such general comparisons. If services are positively related to growth, it seems questionable that growth becomes the harbinger of declining productivity. The confusion inherent in such a perception must await further analysis.

The third hypothesis referred to by Castle and Findley "stresses changes in the nature of industrial organization and business practices" (1988, 5). This hypothesis, which those authors appear to favor, sees services as representing "a way of doing business in relation to the activities of either firms or households" and this way of doing business (the service sector) "grows more rapidly because it pays to do business in new ways as the economy develops" (5).

Robert Stern and Bernard Hoekman saw the share of service employment as "partly a function of structural changes in the 'environment' which can be interpreted as reflecting the development of the economy over time" (1988, 34). In that regard they cited various contributing factors, prominent among which were the changing employment situation with respect to women and the increasingly urbanized population. Accompanying those phenomena over time, they saw increases in specialization as services are moved out of both firms and households and also technological change that leads to what they called "the splintering phenomena" which they described as the unbundling of services from goods. Other factors cited by Stern and Hoekman as contributing to increasing service employment were the expansion of part-time service jobs, the rise of the welfare state, and "the increasing importance of international trade and investment" (34).

Despite the obviously increasing prominence of services on the world scene, Michael Porter observes that controversy exists concerning the importance to individual nations of international success in services as compared to a similar achievement in manufacturing (1990, 266). Porter feels that service ascendancy and success are important in that context. "Many services offer prospects for high levels of productivity and rapid productivity growth" (266). Porter goes on to point out that "many international service industries employ highly skilled workers and managers at home in fields tied to modern technology" (267). Among the examples, he lists custom software as well as consulting and engineering services. He sees various services operating at the cutting edge of technology that are as a consequence essential to the success of various other high-technology industries (267). International service successes in the vein that Porter has in mind lead to an influx of profit from a rather modest investment base as compared to manufacturing (267).

Porter, of course, is more concerned with international competitiveness than with development per se — still he recognizes that various service firms do provide needed expertise, not to mention support for many industries. In this view he is not alone. Economists have been aware of the importance of various services to manufacturing for some time. Beyond that, the linkages that services provide in manufacturing chains add jobs to national economies while, at the same time, providing a certain amount of stability (McKee, 1988, 23). "As the ebb and flow of industrial activities takes place, with varying effects across the map, these service activities generally maintain the flexibility to shift to accommodate the needs of new leading industrial sectors" (23). Thus services appear to have extended a role of flux to actual growth processes by encouraging expansion and perhaps cushioning industrial decline (23).

Once services emerged as facilitators in both the operation and expansion of modern economies, the extension of that role beyond national boundaries was all but inevitable. Indeed the world economy as it exists today would hardly have been feasible at all without a major contribution on the part of various cadres of sophisticated services. Notable among such services are those related to transportation and communications. Without the expansion and continuing improvement of those service subsectors over the past 20 years, the world economy as it exists today would not have emerged.

The importance of services on the world scene is signalled by increasing concern on the part of the signatories of the General Agreement on Tariffs and Trade with respect to emergent difficulties associated with international trade in services. Today services are not merely facilitating various operations in the international economy. They themselves are being traded in that economy. More specifically, services have assumed a major role in the international economy. In facilitating business internationally, in many cases they themselves have become internationalized.

Various purveyors of sophisticated services have contributed to what Porter has termed the internationalization of competition in service pursuits — a phenomenon which he perceives to be on the rise (1990, 250). Porter cites an international similarity of service needs among the factors driving this new competition. In this regard he sees firms in various jurisdictions requiring high-level forms of business service (266). The firms supplying such services, Porter suggests, can easily tailor their offerings to local needs thus keeping a competitive edge over potential competitors in host countries. No doubt since the world has been made smaller in a practical sense through the advances in transportation and communications alluded to earlier, the competitive needs of international service providers have prompted such enterprises to expand the menu of jurisdictions housing and disseminating the services they offer. Clearly this competitively generated pattern of service facilities will have implications for the jurisdictions that host them as well as for those that do not. The general implications for the world economy may have been hinted earlier. Beyond roles associated with facilitating business in the world economy, these services may be increasing their involvement in particular jurisdictions in that economy.

According to Porter, international competition in services has also been heightened by purchasers who are more mobile and better informed (1990, 251). In this regard he alluded to a "more fluid movement of information . . . fast transportation and increasing ease and familiarity with international travel," all of which make "buyers more likely to seek out the world's best service firms" (251). This of course should encourage a further proliferation of service establishments run by international service firms. The market potential of domestic service firms in various locations may be impeded since "buyers with a more international outlook are increasingly willing to hire leading foreign firms operating in this nation" (251).

Porter sees economies of scale in international service firms. These he suggests allow the firms in question "to spread the cost of technology development, training infrastructure, and other activities over worldwide sales revenues" (1990, 251). Other scale economies seen by Porter include the ability to service clients anywhere, worldwide brand recognition, and better scope for utilizing specialized personnel and facilities. Despite Porter's perceptions concerning the ascendancy of international services, he feels that there are still major quality and cost differentials among nations with respect to various services and thus "the state of development of the service sector is very different in different countries" (252).

By focusing on the drives that encourage the expansion of the private sector in market-driven economies and suggesting how such drives have encouraged the growth of international services in the world economy, Porter has broadened the search for an understanding of service roles in an international context. Certainly more knowledge of how services are traded internationally would be helpful to those concerned with international economic and business relations. However, beyond the causes of the international proliferation of services and the institutional and political difficulties associated with trade in services lies another set of issues. Those issues concern the role of services in the international economy and their impacts on the domestic economies that host them. No doubt those impacts can be expected to differ between services as well as between jurisdictions.

In various service subgroups, Porter's view of the rise of international service firms appears to be accurate. If services that are required in the international economy are supplied in large measure by such firms, that of course will have ramifications in constituent domestic economies. In various Third World jurisdictions, for example, it may be that certain international services will only locate as dictated by the competitive needs of the firms concerned as they seek to satisfy their customers, who are themselves in many cases multinational firms. In other words, the establishment or proliferation of certain business services that are international in scope in the specific Third World jurisdictions depends upon the current external linkages that the economies in question possess and to a much more modest degree upon the future potential for such linkages. The day-to-day needs of the economies in question are far down the chain of causality with respect to the ascendancy of the type of services in question. What such jurisdictions can or should do on a policy level to generate such services to attend to domestic needs remains to be seen.

Writing in 1988, Thierry J. Noyelle and Anna B. Dutka suggested that "aside from the periodic reporting by the business press on individual law firms, advertising agencies, consulting houses, or accounting firms, business services remain poorly understood" (9). The reason for such a lack of understanding, they suggest, lies with the fact that until very recently business services were regarded as having emerged to meet the needs of "a selected group of large corporate customers and were not particularly significant for the broader economy" (9). Using the U.S. Standard Industrial Code they defined business services to include the business service group comprised of such components as advertising; computer and data processing, together with consulting and public relations; the legal services' group; and a miscellaneous services group, including (among other things) engineering, architectural and surveying services, accounting, auditing, and bookkeeping services (10).

According to Noyelle and Dutka, no official estimates of the world market for business services exist (1988, 10). Despite that, they suggest that in the immediate post–World War II period "business services grew from being mostly peripheral industries to become increasingly critical components in the workings of business" (25). Indeed they saw business services together with various other service pursuits at the center of the structural transformation that signalled the advent of the "post industrial economy" (25).

Noyelle and Dutka saw the shift toward services in the economy of the United States as meaning that goods are now being produced in that nation in much different ways from what had been the case historically. Such changes in production methods brought with them a greater need for "white-collar personnel and for intermediate service inputs" (1988, 27). The input that they envisioned included transportation and communications, wholesaling, banking and finance, and business services (27). They saw the demand for such services growing as they became "an increasingly integral part of the new ways of doing business" (28). Using auditing services as an example, they suggested that those activities have brought about better accounting control systems and as a consequence, improved control of productive efficiency. Another factor that they cited as stimulating the expansion of business services was "the increasing externalization of service functions by user firms" (28). In this regard they pointed to law and accounting firms as effective suppliers of tax expertise.

Clearly Noyelle and Dutka saw the changing needs of large manufacturing corporations as the proximate cause in the expansion of the service cadres that they identified. They posited this causal linkage in the international sphere as well — "the industrial multinationals paved the way for the business service multinationals" (1988, 29). Speaking of the movement of U.S.-based service firms into foreign jurisdictions, they suggested that such firms frequently discovered that local firms had very little expertise and that as a consequence "U.S. firms played a key role in many countries in creating a domestic market" (29). If their observations are correct, such firms undoubtedly have had a good deal to do with the structure and perhaps the growth or development of the economies in question.

Unfortunately the overall impact of services that are international in nature upon host jurisdictions may be rather difficult to measure because "a whole range of services crosses international boundaries within transnational corporate systems and are typically provided by the parent corporation" (United Nations, 1987, 22). Included in such operating procedures from time to time are such things as advertising, accounting, management, research, data processing, and legal services. Knowledge concerning the extent of such activities may be jealously guarded by the corporations concerned. Thus host jurisdictions may be hard pressed in assessing this impact locally. In addition, the internalized services of international business units may preclude the development of domestic service groups in some cases, resulting in unmeasurable influences upon the economies concerned.

The report suggests that "knowledge of transnational corporations in services still lags behind that of goods-producing transnational corporations" (1987, 23). The report went on to state that "knowledge is still inadequate about their numbers, business strategies, factors accounting for transnationalization, geographical spread, role in the process of transnationalization of the world economy, or their impact on host countries and international transactions" (23). The report attributed these shortcomings in part to the poor quality of data, the relative smallness of international service companies compared to those in manufacturing, and to various "methodological and conceptual problems" (23).

In assessing service impacts in host jurisdictions, it may be important to distinguish between trade and foreign direct investment. As the report points out, services can be difficult to transport, thus necessitating the on site presence of the suppliers (1987, 23). "In some cases this may mean access to the national distribution system . . . in others, it may mean that the foreign suppliers should have the right to sign distribution contracts" (23).

Unquestionably such arrangements will have significant impacts upon host countries. Such impacts may be more noticeable in smaller and developing economies. The impacts in question will be more or less significant, depending upon whether or not the services are aimed at the domestic economy directly or have as their principle focus the world economy. Even services aimed directly at the world economy may have significant impacts on small, local economies (McKee and Tisdell, 1990). Many small, Third World jurisdictions are relying upon services aimed at international markets as vehicles for local expansion. Although some success in such ventures appears evident, a general endorsement of such development programs must await further evidence.

In some cases, exposure to certain business-related services is initiated or enhanced as such services are positioned to meet the needs of the production units of multinational firms. In locations where such production units are positioned to focus upon local markets, the impact of the service groups that they generate may be considerable. If such service groups are themselves international in nature, service-operating modes may bear a foreign stamp, which, depending upon the size and influences of the implanted service establishments, may have considerable impact upon the shaping of the local business service sector and the local economy in general.

One way in which such impacts can occur is through the strategy of international service firms, whereby they diversify their activities into related or even unrelated fields (United Nations, 1987, 30). In this regard, international service conglomerates have been emerging while at the same time industrial firms have been developing service components (30). Services in many cases are being supplied in new markets through foreign direct investment rather than trade. The difference in importance between the two supply vehicles varies between service subsectors (33). Service categories where direct foreign investment is more important include such pursuits as "rental and leasing, advertising, accounting, insurance, data processing services, engineering, trading, hotels, eating and drinking places, oil and gas field services, employment agencies, and electric, gas and sanitary services" (33). The same report saw exports prevailing in travel, franchising, licensing, education, and legal services.

The service sector has been seen as attracting "a significant and increasing share of the flows of the foreign direct investment in the world economy" in recent years (United Nations, 1987, 60). Such flows to developing countries were noticeable but less significant than those between developed economies. The UN report sees factors that affect decisions to invest in services, asserting significant impacts upon the size and direction of overall flows of direct foreign investment (60). It goes without saying that this perception, if accurate, will have major impacts upon the direction of development in various Third World jurisdictions. Thus planners in such jurisdictions may do well to apprise themselves of the direction that the international service sector appears to be taking.

The UN report suggests that Third World host nations have been exerting influences upon foreign direct investment in services through conscious policy directives (1987, 61). However, the utility of such initiatives requires a case-by-case appraisal since the preconceptions of policy-makers with respect to service impacts may be involved. "Traditionally, the risks of permitting investment by service transnational corporations have been perceived by host countries as larger and potential benefits as lower, than those arising from industrial transnational corporations" (61). Service-related investments are often perceived to be less helpful to the balance-of-payments than those geared to exports or import substitution (61). Fears with respect to encouraging new technologies have also been recognized (61). Whether or not potential host nations can or should impact the expansion of international services within their boundaries must be considered by the policymakers in each nation on a case-by-case basis.

Various services are necessary if a particular nation wishes to maintain or increase its participation in the international economy. Of course such a policy commitment may alter the domestic economy of the nation concerned in ways that may be irrevocable but that may be in keeping with the nature of any change that occurs in a profit seeking economy (McKee, 1991). In some nations where the availability of sophisticated cadres of business services is limited, development processes may be adversely affected (United Nations, 1987, 61).

There may be Third World jurisdictions that may not have the option of rejecting the location of international business services. To the extent that such services are facilitators of international business, they may not be needed in specific locations. In a profit motivated international economy, international services will presumably limit their facilities to locations that are potentially profitable.

This of course raises the question as to whether or not governments or, more specifically, planning agencies should consider implanting various services that the international market economy has not generated. In the case of specific services, those involving transportation and communications for example, government involvement may be necessary. However, in other cases there may be little that governments can do.

There is little doubt that "through the use of transportation and communication services, many firms and industries have been able to make dramatic shifts in their operations" (McKee, 1991). These changes are certainly expanding the options of multinational manufacturing concerns with respect to locating facilities in Third World settings. With these expanding industrial options, the development potential of various Third World nations is changing. With these changing options comes the need for more and better services related to business. Third World jurisdictions faced with such opportunities will be hard pressed to reject more substantial linkages to the international economy. With those linkages will come a continuing infusion of investment in international services and still stronger international linkages. In sum, the price of development for Third World economies may be a growing involvement in the world economy and less domestic control of their economic affairs. This option, however unpalatable it may seem to some, may not have been available prior to the relatively recent rise of a sophisticated international service sector.

5

Accounting Services and Economic Development

In initiating a discussion of the role that accounting services play in the international economy and particularly in Third World jurisdictions, it may be well to review one of the factors alluded to by Leslie Castle and Christopher Findlay in support of their argument that service ascendancy parallels economic growth (1988, 4). In stressing that relationship they claimed, among other things, that services represent "a way of doing business in relation to the activities of either firms or households . . . [that] grows more rapidly because it pays to do business in new ways as the economy develops" (5).

This view of services may elicit little discussion within a general overview of forces involved in service ascendancy. However, when applied to specific services, those supplied by international accounting firms, for example, it may prove to be quite helpful. Anthony G. Hopwood (1989, 9) suggested that "accounting has never been a purely national phenomenon," and went on to point out that "both its techniques and the significances that are in part created by them have a history of penetrating national boundaries, moving along the pathways established by commerce and patterns of political influence." Certainly this description put forward by Hopwood appears to be in harmony with what Castle and Findlay have suggested.

International accounting services have grown in keeping with the needs of international business or, perhaps more accurately, in keeping with the needs of the international economy. In doing so there is little doubt that they have influenced the direction of its components both territorial and economic. From the point of view of the firms themselves, recent practice has seen more interest being shown in the international aspects of their practice and, as might be expected, has heightened interest in standardization and harmonization (Hopwood, 1989, 1).

In assessing this heightened interest in international considerations, Hopwood cites various causal inputs. Included are such things as the internationalization of business and the rise of financial markets independent of particular nations (1989, 1). Also considered as important were the interests of "supra-national institutions" wishing to encourage equality with respect to "the conditions of trade and competition" and thus focusing on national variations in forms of economic calculation and on the availability of public information on business units (1). The lesson to be learned appears to be the need for international unification or integration of accounting procedures and standards that if achieved, would have obvious implications for the world economy and its constituent parts.

International considerations are clearly impinging upon accounting procedures in advanced economies. Allan Cook (1989, 33) has listed a number of elements contributing to pressure for accounting change. He cited the possible emergence of a new business practice that may require new concepts or more precise calculations. He also suggested that "general economic and financial conditions may so change that previous assumptions may no longer be maintained," and referred to a movement to floating exchange rates and sustained moderate-to-high inflation as example scenarios that can occur in what he called "major economies" (33). Another cause of change suggested by Cook "may reflect primarily new levels of accountability either voluntarily adopted or imposed by a regulatory authority" (33). In classifying changes in accounting practices, Cook suggested that it would also be possible "to inquire how far change is responding to what one might call a 'real world' problem for the enterprise or country concerned and how far it merely represents standardization for its own sake" (33).

As accounting emerges on the stage of an increasingly integrated and perhaps standardized world economy, more and more inroads will undoubtedly be made into traditional ways of performing accounting functions in individual countries. Accountants are already aware that the setting of accounting standards cannot ignore cultural differences between nations (Bloom and Naciri, 1989) and that the impact of culture on accounting must be considered (Perera, 1989). Beyond that, they are also aware that certain international accounting standards may be inappropriate in developing nations (Hove, 1989). Such an awareness may present a dilemma for accountants and economists alike. There is little doubt that standards and practices that seem to be essential in the international economy and in fact are a part of that economy may be rejected or abridged because of their strangeness to specific domestic economies and, in their own turn, may abridge economic progress in the nations concerned. Of course Third World nations with rich cultural traditions are at specific risk in this regard. If they resist, development may be stifled, and if they acquiesce, it may not be without serious costs in terms of valued traditions and cultural identity.

In economic terms, standardization can have both positive and negative impacts. In the case of accounting services in an international context, standardization can bring with it economies-of-scale that can result in lower costs and perhaps greater profit potential. Standardization may make various personnel and procedures interchangeable, thus allowing for greater flexibility within the accounting firms. Such flexibility may allow the firms in question to shorten their response time with respect to expanding or contracting their operations in specific locations in response to perceived needs for their services.

From the client point of view, standardization means that what the firm can provide throughout the various areas within which it operates can be regarded as a given. Thus those with a potential need for accounting services can assume that those services will be provided within reasonable parameters of quality by the international firm that they select. Of course, this type of client conditioning will heighten international competition between the accounting firms themselves.

Presumably such heightened competition should contribute to the overall efficiency of the industry. Because the nature of basic accounting services — auditing for example — may actually contribute more momentum to the international standardization referred to above, it may make certain forms of competitive behavior on the part of accounting firms difficult. Clients searching for acceptable international uniformity in basic accounting services leave the purveyors of those services with far less scope for product differentiation. It seems clear that, in the case of basic accounting services, real and potential clients have very definite leverage over the nature of the services provided.

Constrained by the standardized basic needs of their international clientele, the accounting firms have found it necessary to seek out channels of competition beyond basic product differentiation. Forms of competition adopted have embraced both the development of new service product lines and the development of new territorial markets. In the case of by-products or new business service offerings, firms whose traditional business base was in auditing have moved into such areas as tax advising, economic and managerial consulting, and forecasting. Through diversifying their offerings, they increase their potential for acquiring new clients for their auditing divisions.

The negative side of standardization is related to inflexibilities that may impact both clients and host jurisdictions. Clients in specific areas may find that they are having to adjust to the ways of the international accounting firms. As such enterprises strengthen their base in specific areas, local firms may be absorbed by them or in some cases may find themselves out of business for lack of customers. Of course it can be argued that the gains from the standardization offered by the international firms far exceed any real or imagined local inconveniences. Particularly in Third World jurisdictions, the confidence that the presence of standardized accounting procedures can instill may act as a stimulus to both local and international business pursuits. In effect the firms and their procedures may contribute both to business confidence and to subsequent expansion and thus to the processes of growth and development themselves. The downside may be a real or perceived loss of economic sovereignty on the part of specific jurisdictions.

Summarizing the causes of accounting change, Cook (1989, 34) cites "new business practices, changes in the financial and economic environment, and new levels of accountability"; with respect to the needs of international business, he saw the coming of microcomputers and improvements in communications as permitting "an upsurge in new forms of financial instruments on a scale that would have been unthinkable a few years ago" (35). Citing the rise of currency swaps during the 1980s, he suggests that the scale of such business has "created an industry within the international banks" that he sees as having a potential for far-reaching impacts "as the market for the original deals becomes saturated and their inventors turn their attention to new and riskier schemes" (35). Other new areas of business that he cites include the rise of futures markets and potential for arbitrage between them and stock markets. Of course, international accounting firms may have valuable services to offer to those involved in such machinations.

As Cook suggested, financial innovations are often responses to various forms of legislation or taxes imposed by national governments. On the international level such innovations may be designed to assist various businesses in navigating the mine fields of taxes and restrictions. It would appear as though successful navigation in such circumstances generally requires considerable accounting inputs that can be provided either internally to multinational firms or externally through the services of international accounting firms. Thus it appears that the accounting firms in question fit the role of facilitator, which has been attributed to business services in general (McKee, 1988). It also appears that it is in that role that the international accounting firms have been able to expand their service offerings beyond what had traditionally been their preserve.

According to Cook, as accounting and reporting procedures themselves become regulated, financial innovations emerge that are designed to bring about needed accounting or disclosure treatments (1989, 36). He cites "off balance sheet finance" as an example of a procedure that is easily transferable between countries, presuming adjustments to deal with the specifics of regulatory roadblocks. Such procedures may render various attempts at international regulation less effective and, by so doing, may contribute further to the integration and strength of the supranational economy. Certainly international accounting firms could hardly eschew interests in such practices and, beyond that, may have to adjust domestic procedures in certain jurisdictions in response to what is occurring.

More and more the provision of accounting services in the world economy has become the preserve of large international firms. In developed nations, concentration appears to be increasing in the accounting industry. In the case of the United Kingdom, it has been suggested that the expansion of larger accounting firms has generated a three-tiered size structure (Daniels et al. 1988, 319). Daniels and his associates go on to say that the upper level is composed of large firms "all of which possess a national network of offices, many with extensive networks" (319). At the lowest level, "the local and specialized nature of the services provided by the small accounting practices means that as yet they are largely unaffected by the market expansion of the larger firms" (320). It seems unlikely that smaller firms of the sort referred to above will have much to contribute to the international economy. Although the logic of Daniels et al. suggests a parallel role for small firms in Third World economies, the reality may be that the emergence of the large, international competitors in such local markets may absorb or eliminate small, independent operations.

Daniels, Leyshon, and Thrift submit that a survival strategy for firms facing competition from upper level firms in the United Kingdom may involve "finding niches in the accounting market, such as sub-contract work on accounting records for larger firms which prefer to concentrate on more lucrative consultancy and advisory work" (1988, 320). They also suggest that specialization in particular market sectors may prove a survival option. The survival potential of smaller, Third World firms through such strategies must be assessed on a case-by-case basis.

In an industry that appears to be becoming increasingly concentrated, Daniels, Leyshon, and Thrift suggest that the importance of such concentration and internationalization "is matched by the increased diversity of accounting services" (1988, 324). In emphasizing this diversity, they state that "large accounting firms are willing to consider setting up in any area of services that will earn fee income" (324). Their analysis of conditions in the United Kingdom sees a decline in the relative importance of fees from auditing. They suggest that the stabilization of the auditing market has actually encouraged accounting firms to cut back upon their reliance on it as an income source — a circumstance that they suggest has coincided with a substantial expansion of demand for a wide menu of consulting and advisory services (324).

Of course such a change in how large accounting firms earn their rewards in a nation state like the United Kingdom has implications for how they may wish to function in the world economy. As important as their traditional auditing functions will undoubtedly continue to be in that economy, it seems likely that the large accounting firms will be becoming even more important players in the international arena if they increase their emphasis upon consulting and advisory services. Through the application of those services, they may impact the direction of a diversity of client groups and thus the direction of the supranational economy as well. This being the case, constituent jurisdictions within the world economy would do well to increase their understanding of the role and potential impact of the firms in question. This seems especially true for Third World jurisdictions, where the firms may have a far broader significance with respect to the paths that growth may take than may have been perceived in the past. A proper understanding of such potential influences should be sought with the specifics of the individual jurisdictions in mind.

In Great Britain, Daniels, Leyshon, and Thrift found that a decline in the overall client base coupled with recessionary impacts have generated stagnation in the audit market, a coincidence of circumstances that they identified as increasing competitive pressures (1988, 324). According to them, "audit work still remains the single most important area of practice, although it is increasingly contributing less than 50 per cent of total fee income in many firms" (325).

It seems unlikely that new service lines of the sort described by Daniels, Leyshon, and Thrift will ever replace basic accounting services such as auditing as the linchpin of the offerings of the international accounting firms in the world economy. However, the broadening of the menu of offerings by those firms will undoubtedly adjust the overall impact that they can be expected to have in the world economy. The same can be said, of course, for the components of that economy, particularly those which make up the Third World.

As mentioned earlier (Chapter 4), economists have been aware that various services make important contributions to manufacturing processes. Historically many such services functioned within the framework of the manufacturing firms themselves. Although many firms that are involved in manufacturing processes still rely on expertise internal to their operations for various service needs, more and more specialized service firms are emerging that are designed to meet the needs of various business interests. Beyond the jobs that are actually housed in such service enterprises, the services themselves, through the linkage functions that they perform, add jobs to national economies and, on the international playing field, to the world economy as well. There is no reason to suppose that such services will not impact Third World jurisdictions. Clearly the international accounting firms are providing various services of the type under discussion here. Thus it must be presumed that they can and do have a role in developmental processes.

Services as facilitators are nowhere more evident than in the fields of transportation and communications. Without the improvements and expansion that have occurred in those service groups, it is fair to say that the integrated world economy that has emerged would not have been possible. Like multinational manufacturing firms, the international accounting firms have benefitted from those innovations. Without the level of economic integration that has emerged in the international economy, the accounting firms could not have become major international players. Certainly roles for them in many Third World jurisdictions might have been slow in emerging.

Despite their presumed dependence upon other service groups, the international accounting firms themselves supply services not just to manufacturing firms operating in the international economy, but to other service firms as well. Indeed, although it may be thought that the accounting firms follow their clients in the manufacturing sector in expanding geographically, real world data do not bear this out. A recent study of the 16 largest international accounting firms lists services of the financial variety as an industry group accounting for more than 50 percent of sales or assets audited worldwide for 13 of the firms under review. For 6 of the firms, the financial industry group accounted for more than 70 percent of sales or assets audited worldwide (Bavishi, 1989, H-3H). That same study shows various other service groups among the clients of the international accounting firms and displays various manufacturing activities as being of relatively modest direct importance to the accounting firms.

Of course if manufacturing pursuits use the offerings of various financial service firms, not to mention other service groups, that in turn utilize the accounting firms in question, linkages, however indirect, still exist. Thus it seems quite clear that the accounting firms are at the center of the cadres of service facilitators that function in advanced domestic economies and in the world economy as well. Their traditional auditing function contributes an order to the economies within which it is provided. That order involves parameters for the reporting and classifying of business and financial data that permit those in need of such data to function more confidently. The argument that the internationalization of accounting services by large multinational manufacturing firms reduces the importance of the international accounting firms is an oversimplification. The firms in question provide services for a wide variety of business and financial service firms, which the manufacturing sector employs extensively.

There seems to be little doubt concerning the important role that the international accounting firms have developed in the world economy through their auditing functions. The introduction of additional services, such as the various forms of consulting alluded to earlier, can only increase their influence. It goes without saying that the basic services of international accounting firms can have strong impacts in Third World economies where they are established. If basic accounting services can increase the operating efficiency of such economies, the new consulting services may have an even more visible impact. The latter type of impact may take the form of increased interest on the part of international economic players seeking to reduce their overall tax bills, avoid various regulations prevalent in developed economies, or reduce general operating expenses. In some cases the consultation services being offered by the accounting firms may even be engaged by governmental agencies. Any or all of the scenarios alluded to here will undoubtedly impact the growth prospects of Third World economies. It seems almost tautological to suggest that host governments, potential private clients, and of course the accounting firms themselves should benefit from a continuing awareness and an increasing understanding of those real or potential impacts.

At this juncture it seems fair to ask why international accounting firms elect to enter particular Third World jurisdictions, particularly those that are among the smallest and poorest. Of course any decision to expand must be tied in some way to continuing or increasing the profits of the firm in question. Whether or not proposed Third World offices must be immediately profitable, profitable over some specified start-up period, or run because of their perceived impact upon the firm internationally will, of course, be both firm and destination specific. Whether the firm in question chooses to buy up an existing local firm, set up some sort of working arrangement with a local firm that will retain its own identity, or open up its own local office will have a bearing on the decision with respect to the treatment of profit potential.

Beyond the immediate question of profits, accounting firms will enter new jurisdictions to retain established international business accounts. As is the case with any supplier of business services, the accounting firms must be sensitive to the needs of their established clients. As those clients expand into new locations, the accounting firms must extend their service networks or risk losing clients to competitors that do. Thus it would appear that many decisions to expand are driven by the need on the part of the firms to maintain their international competitive positions. These types of pressures are reinforced by the desire that seems normal in business organizations to extend the markets for what they have to offer as well as to facilitate their overall operations in the international economy.

In the face of the presumed tendency for the international accounting firms to expand into Third World locations, it seems fair to ask what impact they may have in such jurisdictions. As mentioned earlier, if they result in standardized reporting methods in business, they may generate gains in the efficiency of the economy. Through a demonstration effect, local business may adopt their various procedures, thus strengthening the organization of the market-oriented sector of the economy. Of course the international accounting firms may force smaller domestic operations out of business. To some extent personnel from such local firms may be absorbed by the international competitors, assuming that they meet acceptable standards of expertise. The coming of the international accounting firms may signal better linkages with the international economy that may stimulate certain types of business and thus economic development.

If the firms in question begin providing the various consulting services alluded to earlier in this discussion, they will add to the impacts that they are having on Third World host jurisdictions. Their consulting services may aid in the location and operation of multinational business units in the nations concerned. They may help the operations of domestic firms and may also provide useful expertise to various governmental agencies. All of the kinds of consulting innovations mentioned here will impact the host economies. It may be that such impacts will be relatively greater on the smaller and poorer economies.

Of course, both the auditing and consulting activities of international accounting firms will have impacts upon the world economy and the multinational firms that operate in it. Even in the case of multinationals that make no direct use of the accounting firms, indirect impacts will occur if the activities of accounting firms alter the economies of various Third World jurisdictions in ways that make them more attractive to the multinationals in question.

The situation with respect to accounting firms recalls the work of Michael Porter referred to earlier in this book. Porter cited an international similarity of service needs and saw firms in various locations requiring high-level forms of service (1990, 226). He felt that the international suppliers of such services could easily fit their offerings to the requirements of specific locations, thus besting local competitors. Clearly the menu of services offered by the international accounting firms appears to fit Porter's description.

As was suggested for business services in general, the competitively generated array of accounting service facilities will have implications for jurisdictions that host them as well as for those that do not. In the latter case, those concerned with the basic economic potential of their countries should apprise themselves of why the services in question are not emerging. It is quite possible that some locations may have no demand for such services. In other cases the regulatory climate may be set against them specifically or against the type of activities that are normally perceived to require the services of the accounting firms. In such cases those concerned with development strategy may do well to review the institutional and legislative framework that they are facing, if not supporting. Such a reexamination is especially important if Porter's observations that there are major quality and cost differentials between jurisdictions and that those differentials in turn point to differences in the state of service development (1990, 252) apply to accounting services.

6

The Impact of
Nontraditional Services

In the preceding chapter it was suggested that international accounting firms in an effort to maintain a competitive edge have been developing new product lines as well as new geographical markets. Firms whose traditional preserve was the auditing function are now supplying what seems to be a growing number of additional services. Although the types of services in question may be supplied individually or in groups in various locations by nonaccounting professionals or consultants, they have become strong by-products of the international accounting firms.

As referred to in Chapter 5, the services in question may include such things as tax advising, various forms of economic and managerial consulting, and forecasting. The main constraints in the way of a further expansion of offerings are those normally associated with the international market and the ingenuity and inventiveness of the firms themselves. Of course a continuing expansion of such service menus may pose concern for those within the accounting fraternity who may wish to preserve the position of more traditional accounting functions among the offerings of the firms, but that is not the immediate concern of the current discussion. Instead an attempt will be made to assess the potential impacts of the new service offerings of the accounting firms upon Third World host jurisdictions and upon the international economy.

The facilitating role of traditional accounting services has been referred to earlier (Chapter 5). The addition of new service lines to the offerings of accounting firms represents a clear expansion in their roles as facilitators. Customers for those services abound in the international economy, running the gamut of various multinational firms, wealthy investors, and even governmental agencies in some cases. As the firms go about their business of supplying the needs of such a diverse clientele, it seems clear that they are deepening the integration of the international economy and hopefully may be making it more efficient. Their involvement appears to have major implications for all of the components of that economy, be they clients of the firms in question or not.

The diversity of services being offered by the large international accounting firms can be seen in recent personnel advertisements in *The Economist*. An advertisement placed by Coopers & Lybrand Deloitte proclaimed that the firm "has one of the most successful Construction and Property teams in Management Consultancy" and went on to explain, "Our success is due to the skills of our consultants who are from a variety of backgrounds in the Construction and Property industry" (May 12, 1990, 7).

The scope of that particular firm's offerings becomes more evident as the advertisement continues. "To carry out our increasing range of economic and regeneration studies and strategy assignments we require additional economists, analysts and urban geographers" (*The Economist*, 1990, 7). Noting that their assignments are as varied as their clients, they called for applicants experienced in the areas of "property and construction, town planning or economic development." The advertisement seemed to be aimed at the provision of the services in question within the domestic economy of the United Kingdom, but there is little to suggest that the firm in question and its competitors — both domestic and foreign — could not offer such a menu of services in the international economy, not to mention Third World jurisdictions. It is also clear that governmental agencies may well be major clients for the services in question. Thus such services may play major roles in developmental scenarios in many economies, and the firms supplying them are major players in their own right.

The potential for developmental impacts from international accounting firms can be seen in yet another recent advertisement in *The Economist*. "The Agriculture and Development Division of Deloitte & Touche is seeking candidates for the position of Team Leader for the implementation of a large regional development project in Honduras" (July 2, 1990, 7). The advertisement went on to explain that "over a five-year period the project will develop new and expanded services in a wide range of areas including agricultural production, irrigation, credit, marketing, agro industry, extension and community development." The firm was seeking six long-term staffers and "more than 100 person months of short-term input."

The advertisement advised that the team leader would manage expatriate staff and in concert with a local counterpart, "the day-to-day direction of project activities and liaison with [the] Honduran government" (*The Economist*, 1990, 7). Local counterparts are common to many consulting projects in Third World locations. Their role with respect to actual project leadership must be assessed on a project-by-project basis. The impacts of expatriate decision making on the part of production units based in Third World jurisdictions have been known to economists for some time (Parry, 1973; McKee, 1977). In the case of foreign consultants, their impacts should presumably be suited to the needs of the nations concerned if they are hired by governmental agencies of those nations. If they are hired to pursue the interests of multinational firms with interests in particular nations, presumably they will have greater potential for initiating economic impacts less well calibrated to the developmental needs of the host nations.

In the Deloitte & Touche project, it is quite clear that the firm will be working in close cooperation with governmental elements in Honduras. "Technical responsibilities will focus upon institutional analysis and strengthening of the client regional organization and other parastatal agencies operating in the area" (July 21, 1990, 7). In the case of the project in question, the firm, which is based in Canada, appears to be relying upon nonpermanent staffing. Of course firms that rely on temporary staff on a project-by-project basis may not establish credentials with respect to performance over time or between projects. The continuity that comes from permanent staff and centrally determined procedures may not be evident. However, hiring from project to project may carry with it attractive cost-cutting features and greater flexibility. How varying staffing policies actually affect sperformance in the field requires case-by-case appraisal. From the point of view of the firms involved, decisions with respect to permanent versus temporary staffing may hinge upon the current volume of business or opportunities to expand it and upon the availability of employable skills in the international labor markets.

From the anecdotal evidence presented above, it seems clear that the consulting activities of large accounting firms cover a wide range of services. Indeed it seems likely that their operations may encompass almost any aspect of business or economic activity within advanced economies, internationally, or in Third World jurisdictions. Examples of the breadth of consulting projects that are being undertaken by the international accounting firms can be seen in the literature produced by Price Waterhouse for the use of their clients throughout the world. Such offerings include a series of location-specific information guides that provide basic business, economic, and legal overviews of the various jurisdictions within which the firm offers its services.

A general overview of the potential impact of such publications will be provided in due course. For the moment, example guidebooks will be employed as a basis for reviewing the various consultative services that are offered by the firm. In their publication on Fiji, Price Waterhouse announced that the principal services provided by their practice in that island nation included assistance with respect to taxation and exchange control, corporate reconstruction and insolvency, independent business service areas and recruitment, and personnel and training, in addition to their basic audit and accountancy menu (1988, 86).

In elaborating upon what can be done for clients in the area of taxation and exchange controls, the guide states, "Our tax staff has the capability and experience to render a wide range of services, including consultancy on exchange control matters, representation before Exchange Control authorities, preparation of income tax returns, income tax planning, estate and family tax planning, and international tax planning" (Price Waterhouse, 1988, 86). Clearly such services will have an impact upon the jurisdiction within which or concerning which they are offered. By attracting international clients and presumably international financial capital, they will undoubtedly increase the integration of jurisdictions such as Fiji or others, where they are offered successfully, into the international economy.

From the point of view of those jurisdictions, such an integration may provide higher levels of needed foreign exchange, more employment opportunities in the domestic economy, and presumably economic expansion. On the downside, the successful offering of taxation and exchange control services may cause the erosion of a certain amount of economic sovereignty as the economies in question adjust their parameters to become organic parts of a larger entity — the world economy. Those concerned with the domestic integrity and direction of the economies in question will have to assess their priorities, not to mention the costs and benefits accompanying them, on a case-by-case basis. By facilitating the dissemination of advice on such issues to potential and actual clients, Price Waterhouse (in the case of Fiji) and its rivals (in whatever jurisdictions they offer such services) are major facilitators of economic change. It would appear that the potential for gain or loss through such practices can hardly be ignored by Third World governmental agencies, much less by the firms themselves, since the advantages of both will undoubtedly be served best if sound developmental processes and growth patterns are stimulated.

The firms in question may have major roles in legal tax avoidance through the international economy. "Our tax staff also works in conjunction with the audit staff in developing suggestions and plans for minimizing the client's income tax liability" (Price Waterhouse, 1988,

86). In addition, the staff of the firm cited "work with the client in appraising all the appropriate alternatives to ensure that maximum tax benefits are obtained and in dealing with international tax problems" (86).

It would appear that tax matters represent one of the major areas of expanded service offerings on the part of the international accounting firms beyond their basic audit and accountancy functions. Of course, in advanced industrialized economies tax-related services have been among the offerings of accounting firms for some time. Thus it is hardly surprising that this aspect of their operations should take on an even larger relative significance in the preserves of the world economy. In that new and growing environment, the impact of such services seems to be expanding as well. There is little doubt that the accounting firms, through servicing the needs of their clients, are having a very real impact upon the movement of and ultimate positioning of both financial and physical capital resources and hence upon locational strengths in the world economy. An understanding of that reality would appear to be beneficial to those pursuing developmental goals within that economy, especially those concerned with planning courses of expansion for Third World economies.

In their information guide for Fiji, Price Waterhouse have indicated service offerings with respect to corporate reconstruction and insolvency. In that general area, they explain that they aid banks with business reviews designed to assess the future potential and viability of bank customers in financial difficulties (1988, 87). They are careful to indicate that, in dealing with insolvency, they seek to preserve business and generate opportunities. Such aims, when successful, would certainly be a positive influence upon the economy in question. To the extent that Price Waterhouse or other firms are providing such services in Fiji or other Third World economies, they are making direct contributions to the economic stability and to the continuing development of such jurisdictions. Even in cases where the accounting firms prove powerless to prevent specific insolvencies, they may be able to soften the blow for the economy concerned. "If . . . receivership or liquidation is unavoidable, we seek to combine this approach with maximizing realizations for creditors" (87). That the firm itself is cognizant of its opportunity to influence the economy and wishes to do so can be seen in its closing statement on reconstruction and insolvency services, where it declares that its practitioners are desirous of making a positive contribution "by reconstructing and nursing back to viability businesses that are in financial difficulty" (87). Once again the role of the facilitator is very much in evidence.

In the realm of independent business services, Price Waterhouse explains that a significant portion of its Fiji practice is aimed at helping independent businesses with their problems (1988, 87). Their own appraisal of their role in this regard suggests that they are well aware of the impact they may be having. The independent businesses in question "unlike major public companies, do not always have the in-house resources to solve their problems" (87). Thus it can be seen that various services to independent businesses represent yet another area where the accounting firms can have a stabilizing and supportive influence on Third World jurisdictions. Indeed such an influence may prove invaluable in the overall effort towards sustained economic expansion.

According to Price Waterhouse, they are also suppliers of recruitment, personnel, and training services in Fiji. In this regard they accept assignments concerning the recruitment and placement of staff, job evaluation, executive compensation, and salary surveys. All such services may be in short supply in various Third World locations. Thus by making them available, Price Waterhouse or other accounting firms are once again facilitating efficiency in the economies in question. Beyond the services mentioned above, Price Waterhouse, through their practitioners in Fiji, stand ready to assist with acquisitions and mergers, share valuations, feasibility studies, the quantification of difficult insurance claims, and hardware and software evaluation and implementation services (1988, 87–88).

Although Price Waterhouse has operations in a large number of Third World jurisdictions, the services that they offer beyond the traditional accounting and auditing menu appear to vary in keeping with local markets. Some locations may enjoy fewer consulting service options than Fiji while others can conceivably access an even wider array. In Barbados, for example, the Price Waterhouse service menu is somewhat more extensive than its counterpart in Fiji, perhaps reflecting a more extensive integration of the Caribbean economy in question with international interests and perhaps reflecting a more diversified economy with broader service needs.

In Barbados, the firm offers various forms of information technology consulting. Included are such services as system design, selection, and implementation and custom programming. Software sales and local area network installation together with support for those offerings are also on the menu. The firm also performs data security reviews. Beyond its information technology offerings, the firm can provide "corporate administration, in support of offshore companies, including acting as local agent and dealing with staff supervision, reinvoicing and banking needs" (1989, 114). These latter services no doubt reflect the role of Barbados as an offshore business center. Strengthening that supposition is the fact that the firm offers "advice on all aspects of offshore business in Barbados and Antigua" (114). Beyond the services referred to already, it offers trustee and trust administration services, arranges incorporations of companies, and even supplies corporate secretarial services.

It seems quite clear that the wide array of services discussed above, whether offered by Price Waterhouse or its competitors, have great potential for impacting host economies. Large accounting firms in advanced nations are adding to the service sectors in those locations and are insuring a significantly stronger form of economic integration in those economies. As such services expand internationally, they facilitate the operations of multinational manufacturing firms and bring a more strongly integrated international economy into being. When specific destinations are added by individual accounting firms with respect to the more traditional accounting services, competitors undoubtedly feel considerable pressure to expand themselves.

Accounting firms entering new geographical locations with their basic services will then be in a position to expand the types of ancillary services that have been alluded to earlier in this chapter, in keeping with the needs and potential of their new domestic locations and, of course, international conditions. The same competitive conditions that stimulated the expansion of their basic services are once again assuming causal roles in the expansion of consulting activities. To stay competitive, the pressure is directed toward reaching new markets and broadening service offerings.

These changes that have been occurring in the major accounting firms are not being welcomed with unqualified enthusiasm throughout business communities. "As big certified public accounting firms' revenues from management consulting skyrocket, more critics are asking whether accountants can objectively audit business decisions they help make" (Berton and Schiff, 1990, 101). Presumably such questions could be asked concerning the firms' international operations and those in Third World locations as well.

Beyond such basic questions, management-consulting firms may be concerned that the auditors gain an unfair competitive advantage by recommending their own services to clients. Certainly the major international accounting firms with networks of offices in place to do basic accounting functions would appear to have such advantages over consulting organizations seeking to expand in the international market. It may be that the accounting firms with their strong, international linkages may be in a position to best domestic consulting rivals in Third

World locations as well. Their ability to expand into new service lines in such locations may preclude domestic aspirants to consulting activity. Of course looked at from grounds of economic efficiency, such developments are hardly good or bad in and of themselves. If the accounting firms are best equipped to supply such needed services effectively, caveat emptor. The ultimate judgment must await the results of such services in the impacted locations.

Such criticisms notwithstanding, accounting firms are making major incursions into consulting in the United States. Berton and Schiff pointed out that five of the ten top management-consulting firms in this country are accounting firms (1990, 102). "Arthur Andersen & Co. . . . is in first place; Peat Marwick is fifth; and Price Waterhouse, Ernst & Whinney and Coopers & Lybrand are eighth, ninth and 10th, respectively." Berton points to mounting criticism as the firms move into specific consulting pursuits that have been considered "to border on conflict of interest with the auditing side of the business" (102–3). For example, "Peat Marwick recently bought a major share of a public-relations firm. Arthur Andersen has become a major competitor in the asset-appraisal business" (103). Other major firms "are putting heavier emphasis on consulting for investment bankers in corporate mergers, reorganizations and bankruptcies" (103). Berton and Schiff suggest that the accounting profession in the United States should "be careful of where its management consulting business is headed" (104). "When it moves over the line of giving advice to making actual business deals and directing business strategy for audit clients, it may encounter the ire of Congressional watchdogs" (104).

Irrespective of such concerns, it is evident that the new service lines that are emerging in large accounting firms will continue to expand in keeping with the needs of the economies that house them. Real or presumed conflicts with their more traditional functions notwithstanding, the firms in question are in a strong position to offer new service lines within advanced economies, internationally, and in Third World locations. In place networks of offices and accounting practitioners afford a ready base for the firms to expand into new endeavors. Confidence built over years of accounting practice encourages potential consulting clients to approach the firms rather than rival consultants.

Speaking of services in general, Michael Porter saw the basis for the growth of large, multiunit service firms as a "systematization and in some cases standardization of the process of delivering services" (1990, 245). He saw such organizations as capable of replicating services consistently and well in multiple locations by using standardized facilities, operating modes, and procedures to guide employees (28). Porter's portrayal appears to be accurate in terms of the functioning of the accounting firms in the international economy. The factors that have facilitated the emergence of the international accounting firms are seemingly doing double duty with respect to the entry of those firms into the diverse service pursuits that have been the subject of this chapter. Since the firms are presently on site in a vast array of locations internationally, they hold distinct advantages in expanding into wider service lines in those locations. They are also in a strong competitive position to open up in new locations should market conditions seem to recommend such moves.

As seen in the rather wide array of published materials that Price Waterhouse has made available to clients and other interested parties, there are competitive economies to be realized through the dissemination of information as well. By following such practices, the firms are saying we can provide you with a diversity of business information that will stand you in good stead in the world economy. The point would hardly be missed by the users of such information put forward by Price Waterhouse or other firms that those firms are available to provide accounting services and perhaps to facilitate a vast array of operational issues in various international locations. Thus information dissemination is not only a tool for acquiring and servicing clients, it may also channel the operations of those clients to specific locations that are shown to provide the business environments that they are seeking. While the accounting firms are not alone in effecting such channeling, their role in that regard should not be underestimated.

It has been suggested that "international business would not be possible without extensive international trade in services" (Feketekuty, 1988, 18). Indeed, various services are the facilitators that have encouraged the emergence of a better integrated world economy. "If services that are related to business have become facilitators of change in the world economy, as well as in advanced nations, it is to those service subsectors that one must look in attempting to identify a leadership role for services in Third World expansion" (McKee and Tisdell, 1990, 20). If the international accounting firms have been among those facilitating agents because of their basic functions, their potential as facilitators can only have been strengthened by the emergence of their new service offerings. There appears to be little doubt that what they are doing impacts developmental patterns in Third World economies.

They are not alone in their expanding roles as facilitators. "Various sophisticated services, many of which may not be located in Third World nations, are contributing to the feasibility of production facilities in those nations" (McKee and Tisdell, 1990, 29). In the case of the array of consulting services that the accounting firms offer, there is an added advantage in that they may be provided through the local office of the firm in question. In any case, the local office, by its being on site, can serve as a contact point and liaison if the firm's consulting specialists are to be brought in. Of course some may suggest that such practices may bring criticisms to the fore that are similar in nature if not in extent to those alluded to earlier in this chapter relating to potential conflicts of interest. Be that as it may, the physical presence of the international accounting firms in numbers of Third World jurisdictions undoubtedly facilitates the expansion of the firms' consulting functions. Thus it seems evident that the firms are in a position to impact the economies in question in various ways well beyond those described in the discussion of their basic accounting roles (Chapter 5).

Lest it may appear that these impacts are largely felt in manufacturing activities, it must be pointed out that they can emerge in economies where multinational manufacturing firms play minimal roles. Certainly the emergence of various services, including those provided by the accounting firms, has facilitated the installation and growth of industrial facilities in various Third World nations. However, the accounting firms have branches in various Third World nations that are hardly known for their industrial potential. In such locations, it may seem that there will be little scope for the emergence of consulting activities based in accounting firms. It is possible that nodes of sophisticated services, including those housed in accounting firms, may emerge in Third World economies not geared to manufacturing — offshore banking centers, for example, or other nonmanufacturing nations that may be able to market certain services internationally or regionally.

In summarizing the real and potential impacts that consulting services offered by accounting firms have in Third World locations, it seems clear that they are among those services considered to be facilitators of economic activity. By aiding in locational activity, offering various forms of managerial inputs, and aiding business organizations to operate in a rather complicated world economy, they seem to be strengthening the potential for business successes in Third World settings. In large Third World nations, they may have much to contribute to the strengthening, if not the growth, of the domestic economy. Indeed, they may well function in much the same way in such settings as sophisticated cadres of services have been doing in advanced economies where they have been instrumental in facilitating the operations of the manufacturing sector and cushioning economic change (McKee, 1988).

In smaller Third World settings, they may still have parts to play through providing assistance to neighboring nations on a regional basis and by providing specific business expertise to the domestic economies of their host countries. Services that facilitate operations in the world economy may, when housed in smaller jurisdictions, give those locations a role in the international economy that they may not otherwise have had. In short, it would appear that, in consort with other service facilitators, they have much to offer the private sectors of economies that are in the process of developing.

There will be some who contend that such services offered by the large accounting firms will increase the dependence of host nations on the world economy and foreign interests. This of course may be true, but such linkages must always be weighed against the benefits that accompany them. In the case of many small Third World jurisdictions, it may be that foreign linkages may be their only opportunity for economic advancement. In larger settings, the growing consulting menu may impact the domestic economy by providing income and employment directly and indirectly.

Little has been said in the present context concerning the impact of the services in question when they are employed by agencies of host governments. This is a complicated issue that may be best left to the policy section of the current volume. For the moment, suffice it to say that the firms in question may have much to offer host governments in the way of consulting expertise. The extent of potential offerings may be to some extent destination specific.

To generalize, it would appear that the international accounting firms have turned what may have been regarded initially as very secondary service offerings into a rather significant subset of their worldwide business. The fact that expanding consulting services are contributing positively to firm revenues signals that they have acquired a substantial client base. In the Third World, the continuing expansion of these consulting activities should be expected to have increasing impacts upon the economies concerned.

7

Technology and the Impact of International Accounting Firms

Writing in 1987, Stephen S. Cohen and John Zysman referred to a structural change in international markets that has been accompanied by adjustments in the production base found in advanced nations (79). They saw the changes that they envisioned as altering the organization of production, the actual location of production facilities, and "who plays what role in the process" (79). Clearly the internationalization of production is part and parcel of the major structural adjustment envisaged by those authors, and clearly that process has depended for its obvious success upon the major advances in transportation and communications that have been taking place in the latter half of the twentieth century.

Just as the organization of production in advanced nations, the United States, for example, has been undergoing profound adjustments (see Clark, Gertler, and Whiteman, 1986, 12), changes in the international ordering of production that are even more profound have been occurring. Clark and his colleagues cited among pertinent changes within the United States "the verticle integration of sequential functions within single firms and, more recently, a multilocational arrangement of production" (12). It seems obvious that their observations could be applied with little adjustment to the international economy. Indeed it is changes in the nature of production coupled with advances in transportation and communications networks that have made it possible for various Third World locations to participate more fully in the international economy. In consort with the changes alluded to here have come the development of various sophisticated service cadres aimed at facilitating business in the world economy.

There is no evidence to suggest that the spread of production facilities and related services has reached its peak. In the case of the United States, the "spatial transformation of industry which finds new economies of production in spatially discontinuous configurations that defy the old agglomerative forces while still offering the benefits of large firm size" (Clark, Gertler, and Whiteman, 1986, 13) appears to be continuing. The same observation seems to apply to the international economy and to emerging structural adjustments in Third World economies. Large firms can place components of their production processes in numerous locations throughout the world, constrained only by the profit potential of their operations and by the transportation, communications, and other service cadres necessary to realize such potential.

Cohen and Zysman see the changes under discussion here as fueled at least partially by "a technological revolution spreading across major segments of manufacturing services" (1987, 80). The revolution in question they see as based upon wide applications "of new microelectronic-based production, and telecommunication technologies" (80). Cohen and Zysman see what they describe as the beginning of a new industrial era. In this regard they have suggested that the convergence of computers and the technology of communications is giving birth to a new infrastructure; that the telecommunications equipment and service industries have become strategic industrial sectors; and that the new telecommunications will change competitive processes "among firms in sectors throughout the economy" (181). Although aimed at the United States, their analysis appears to be equally applicable to the international economy and also to Third World locations.

From the perspective of Organization for Economic Cooperation and Development countries, telecommunications technologies are seen as converging rapidly to open up a wide selection of new opportunities for the users and suppliers of networks (Snow and Jussawalla, 1989, 21). The industry is seen as facing "massive upheavals that are challenging established institutional and industrial structures" (21). Snow and Jussawalla go on to suggest that the convergence of computing and communication technologies, affecting industries other than telecommunications, are at the heart of the process that they are describing (21).

Although it is conceded that the marriage between the technology of telecommunications and computers is altering the industrial and business landscape in revolutionary ways, the role of various sophisticated service subsectors in the accelerating processes of change can hardly be ignored. "By extending markets and providing more flexibility in production chains, services have dramatically altered the processes of production" (McKee, 1988, 115). Various services contribute to facilitating the passage of materials, personnel, and financial assets through national boundaries, and it can be said that "a sophisticated cadre of international services has developed to accommodate the needs of the international business community" (115).

If services are facilitating the operations of various industries, it can also be said that at least some of those services may have the industries in question as their sole raison d'être. This can be seen in service configurations that have emerged in various locations throughout the world that house the production facilities of multinational firms. In a very real sense, the services have followed the manufacturing firms to accommodate their needs.

In some ways, services may be considered as integral to the actual functioning of certain industries, despite the fact that they have both an existence and functions that are separate from or transcend the industries in question. Today the linkages between various activities seem to be blurring industrial and sectoral boundaries which were taken for granted twenty years ago. "[T]echnological change has eroded the clear distinctions that existed in the market place" (Robinson, 1988, 42). In support of this contention Robinson points out that computing services were quite distinct from telecommunications that, in turn, were quite distinct from postal services. He goes on to suggest that it is no longer easy to separate banking services from nonbanking services. He points to hotel chains that have entered the teleconferencing business and to department stores that are providing financial services. Beyond that he suggests that banks are becoming electronic publishers and that manufacturers are moving into services (142). In such a business climate it hardly should be surprising if the configuration of accounting services is changing or if accounting firms are moving beyond basic accounting services.

There is little doubt that the adjustments referred to have been encouraged and made possible, if not caused, by technological change. Robinson is of the opinion that "technological change, in addition to affecting markets and products has had profound impacts on the international operations of business" (1989, 43). In that regard he sees functions becoming easily transferable from place to place and labor being replaced by information technology equipment. He sees services being removed from business in some cases while being added in others. Overall he sees the factors alluded to above as generating or bringing about a greater meshing of functions resulting in improvements in productivity as a result of better planning, smaller inventories, and improvements in distribution (43).

The type of meshing alluded to above can be seen in the broadening role taken on by banks in advanced economies. Some see the banks in many such economies as having become major actors in national science and technology systems. Beyond that, they are playing "a part which is at least as important as that of industrial firms, universities, research establishments and government agencies dealing with science and technology" (Jéquier and Yao-Su Hu, 1989). Whether or not accounting firms and other business-related services can claim as central a role with respect to science and technology remains to be seen. In advanced economies, banks may have a more personalized interest in matters technological since, by lending money to technological endeavors, they are at risk if such enterprises fail or if their knowledge of them is inadequate.

In the case of accounting firms there is little doubt that improvements in information processing, the ever increasing role of computers, and continuing improvements in information networking are really the factors that have been so successful in internationalizing their operations. Granted that they require customers to justify their entry into new locations and thus that their international expansion has followed that of manufacturing firms, such growth could hardly have been as successful if the technological adjustments referred to had not been occurring. In that case, manufacturing firms would have had to rely much more heavily upon the accounting services provided by local firms, thus losing the consistency of worldwide services that can only be attained through the homogenized operations and networking of internationalized accounting firms.

Clearly the emergence of such firms and the locational flexibility that technology has provided for them may have dramatic impacts upon the development potential of various Third World settings. Robinson's analysis applies well in the case of accounting firms. The functions of such firms are indeed easily transferable from place to place even if some of the places in question are in the Third World. If the firms can rely on information technology and computerized operating techniques that can be accessed internationally, they can provide a level of service that might have been slow in emerging in settings where basic accounting expertise is in short supply.

Beyond the impact of the technological advances on the expansion patterns of accounting firms are the impacts that those firms may be having in the settings they choose. Many of those impacts have already been highlighted in this book (Chapter 5) and need not be reviewed at this point. However it should be recognized that the technology that brings the firms into Third World settings may provide a demonstration effect in those settings. Its utility may be recognized, and it may be applied in other pursuits. In cases where this occurs, the accounting firms are in a causal role beyond what the basic supplying of efficient international accounting services would seem to suggest and beyond the impact of any basic employment multipliers that may emanate from increasingly efficient accounting services.

Aside from basic accounting services, the expanding range of consulting services (Chapter 6) that accounting firms offer may well have technological impacts upon the economies to which they are applied. Such impacts may be quite extensive, presumably limited only by the extent of consulting services offered and, of course, by the skill of those offering them. In assessing the technological function of banks, Jéquier and Yao-Su Hu saw it "as a side-effect or indirect consequence of . . . activities as a financial intermediary or development institution" (1989, 6). Their appraisal of the banks as technological institutions may be useful in reaching a better understanding of accounting firms in that role. They suggest that banks are seen as technological institutions not because they are in the business of promoting technological innovation but because of their "direct or indirect influence on the rate and direction of a country's technological development, on the technological choices made by industrial firms and the agricultural sector, and on the patterns of technology imports" (6).

In a traditional sense, accounting firms probably have never thought of themselves as technological institutions per se. Nonetheless in their burgeoning consulting offerings they may be moving more in that direction. As in the case of banks, they may have begun moving in that direction as a by-product of their basic business persona or perhaps as a way of reinforcing it.

If today their revenue from consulting is beginning to rival that from traditional accounting operations, they may have to fine tune their self-image as purveyors of technological innovations, depending on the nature and extent of the technological content of their consulting operations. Jéquier and Yao-Su Hu have defined a technological institution to include any organization playing a clearly recognizable part in processes relating to technological innovation whether in the promotion or financing of research or in the development of a country's technological capacities (1989, 6). It would appear as though accounting firms are meeting this perception in Third World settings through both direct and indirect (not explicitly sought) impacts.

"From the point of view of economic growth and development, what matters is not so much scientific and technological activities in laboratories, universities or research centres as the embodiment of technology in investment and production in different sectors of the economy"

(Jéquier and Yao-Su Hu, 1989, 86). It seems clear that accounting firms facilitate such embodiments in various ways. By providing standardized international services to industrial customers, through their own technological networking, and by their capability of setting up in various locations to meet the needs of their customers, they aid in the international transfer of technology, which seems an inevitable accompaniment to the operations of multinational manufacturing firms.

The operating technologies of the accounting firms themselves in Third World settings may demonstrate their utility on a level that renders them marketable to local, nonaccounting businesses. Thus a demonstration effect emanating from the accounting firms themselves may initiate the spread of their own technologies in the economies of host nations. In addition to the above supports to technological development, it seems clear that accounting firms have great scope for influencing technological adjustments in Third World settings through their consulting activities. In that regard they are only limited by how far they are willing to extend the scope of their consulting and by the willingness of customers to utilize their services.

It seems clear that accounting firms operating in the world economy can impact the dissemination of technology in Third World settings and indeed influence the processes of economic development in those settings. On the surface this appears to be a positive feature of the operations of those firms. Clearly they are playing a role in the expansion of Third World economies and in strengthening the linkages of those economies to the rest of the world.

The nature of the accounting firms, whereby they operate through actual facilities in various Third World settings, may enable them to become less a party to aspects of the dissemination of technology that have been criticized by specialists in economic development. Technology and the expertise concerning it that comes from the developed world is thought by some to be suspect in Third World locations. It has been suggested that such technology is often geared to the economic needs of developed nations and "hence tends to be suited to their economic circumstances, which favor large-scale, capital-intensive, often skill-intensive, production" (Forsyth, 1990, 123). Forsyth sees the market for technology as highly monopolistic and suggests that it follows (at least in the case of small, developing countries), that a weak bargaining position with respect to large machinery producers will afford few concessions from the producers in question to the needs or special requirements of the nations concerned. He sees the sellers of technology as holding all the cards (123).

In the case of the accounting firms and perhaps in the case of other service operations, the concerns voiced by Forsyth may not be too significant. The accounting technology that the firms bring to bear in Third World settings has as one of its major advantages its ability to plug into external linkages. Where the firms locate, they may be instrumental in contributing to a business climate conducive to the success of businesses that are looking to world markets as well as those whose major interests are local. Through their consulting activities, the accounting firms may be able to contribute to the adoption of appropriate technologies by their clients, although it should be mentioned that what constitutes appropriate industrial technology in a particular setting lies well beyond the parameters of the present discussion.

If there are arguments for the use of industrial technology that is not on the cutting edge of international standards in Third World settings, those arguments seem far less plausible in the case of various sophisticated services. Even in the medical field where training in advanced nations equips professionals from Third World locations with skills in dealing with conditions more germane to the needs of the developed world, caution is indicated in using that circumstance for arguing that the medical needs of the Third World are less sophisticated. Instead it seems more appropriate to argue that the best medical technology available for dealing with the health problems of Third World jurisdictions should be sought. No one would argue that various vaccinations, inoculations, and other preventive programs should not be used because Third World nations, characterized by surplus labor pools, would be better served by retaining or creating as many job opportunities as possible in the business of caring for those who fall ill.

Forsyth distinguishes between technology per se, which he equates to plant and machinery and technological know-how, which he defines as technological information and skills, which he sees embodied in individuals (1990, 73). Among the individuals who possess the skills in question are scientists and engineers, as well as technical, engineering, and management consultants. He also includes as examples of technological know-how the management of firms and labor skills (73). Technological know-how may also be found "in some impersonal information source such as license or patent documentation, services for disseminating intelligence on technology, technical drawings, publications, seminars, etc." (73). It seems as though much of the business conducted by accounting firms would fit well in Forsyth's classification.

In Forsyth's view the basic functions of know-how in the Third World have to do with the enhancement of technological capability in various spheres (1990, 73). Although the work of accounting firms may fit in this taxonomy, Forsyth, like many economists and development specialists, is not thinking of accounting and other business services in his analysis of technological know-how. What he considers to be important (among other things) is the ability to find and purchase appropriate technologies at reasonable prices and the capacity to assimilate the acquired technology. Beyond these considerations he suggests that it is important to be able to expand or duplicate the technology in question as well as to modify or improve it as necessary. Finally he cited as important "the capability to generate new appropriate technology, probably as a result of local research and development activity" (73).

Jéquier and Yao-Su Hu have a slightly different view. "Technological development is often equated with R&D and with the invention of new products and processes" (1989, 111). If this is what is meant by technological development, those authors seem skeptical of its importance in Third World jurisdictions. "[T]he experience of newly industrialized countries suggests that inventing new products and new processes is not at the center of the technological development work needed for successful industrialisation" (111). Instead what they feel is needed and indeed central is attaining and nurturing "the capabilities needed for making technological choices and for fostering more efficient production and investment performance" (111).

It seems as though the accounting firms make significant contributions to satisfying the needs that Jéquier and Yao-Su Hu have outlined. Both their basic accounting functions and their consulting services would appear to strengthen the climate for business dealings on both the domestic and international levels. Jéquier and Yao-Su Hu suggest that anything that a country has not done before entails something new and involves some learning effect (1989, 111). The accounting firms, by contributing to a systematic record of business dealings throughout host economies, not only contribute to facilitating transactions within those jurisdictions but also make the economies in question and their component enterprises more palatable targets for foreign business linkages. Learning effects from the operation of the firms cannot help but continue to strengthen accounting procedures throughout host economies with the obvious effect of strengthening the economies themselves.

Various students of Third World development have displayed ongoing concerns with respect to foreign linkages that various emerging nations may sustain. In its most extreme form, that point of view suggests that Third World nations have been exploited over time by more fortunate nations and that the road to development must circumvent such exploitation where it still exists. Regardless of what may have been true in the past, a more realistic view may be that all nations with market-oriented economies are part of a world economy, adjustments in which are increasingly in keeping with the needs and operations of multinational firms (McKee, 1991). The welfare of individual economies, whether large or small, rich or poor, is inextricably linked with that world economy. Accounting firms and other purveyors of services that facilitate the operations of both domestic and international business seem destined to contribute to the growth and continuing viability of business interests and presumably may make similar contributions to the economies concerned. Theirs is a service technology that seems indispensable to sound business operations and thus to the strength of the economies that nurture them.

Jéquier and Yao-Su Hu understand that technological independence is hardly a goal worth pursuing on the part of Third World nations. "The experience of the newly industrialized countries . . . suggests that what matters is not technological self-sufficiency, which may entail a heavy price in poor production, but the ability to combine foreign and local technological elements" (1989, 112). They go on to add that the combination suggested should be brought to fruition "in a way that progressively develops local capabilities in areas where they can be deployed in the most efficient way" (112).

It appears that this view of the employment of technology in general applies very well to the hosting of international accounting firms by Third World nations. Such nations may not be self-sufficient in domestic accounting services. The establishment of the international firms will certainly contribute to the local business climate. Beyond that the firms themselves in functioning locally can become a training ground for local accounting talent. At the same time they can interact with local professionals and business interests in ways that will allow them to fine tune their service offerings to meet the needs of the local market. Thus the accounting firms should be able to provide the best of two worlds to their local host economies. They should be able to accommodate the accounting needs of the local economy while, at the same time, offering linkages to local business interests with the world economy through their well-established international channels and standardized procedures.

Beyond that, the firms in question should be able to contribute to the strengthening of their Third World host economies. What Jéquier and Yao-Su Hu have suggested with respect to technology applies to this issue very well. "The acquisition and development of an indigenous technological capability requires conscious efforts over a long period of time" (1989, 112). Such efforts should include the monitoring of what is being done locally "to try out new possibilities, to keep track of new developments throughout the world, to accommodate additional skills, and to increase the country's ability to respond to new pressures and new opportunities" (112). It would appear that all of those goals are well within attainable parameters for the accounting firms. Indeed the promotion of such objectives would appear to be implicit in their operations.

The basic operations of accounting firms contribute to improving the economic climate of Third World economies through diffusion — "an informal process which relates to the transfer of information either in embodied form through movement of personnel, or through interaction between customers and suppliers" (Forsyth, 1990, 74). Clearly knowledge of the operating procedures of accounting firms and internationally acceptable accounting procedures are diffused when the firms hire local personnel, when they deal with local clients, and when former employees acquire positions in local accounting firms where they exist or in firms in other pursuits that can utilize their expertise. It may also be that diffusion occurs through the consulting activities of the accounting firms.

It may be too soon to assess the overall impact of international accounting firms in Third World locations, but it seems clear that they are contributing to the economic linkages of such locations with the world economy. Speaking of the information revolution in financial services, Joan Spero believes "that in the long run information technology . . . will benefit developing countries and will reduce not increase, disparities between the countries of the North and the South" (1989, 112). Perhaps an equally optimistic forecast may apply to the impact of the accounting firms.

III

IMPLICATIONS FOR DEVELOPMENTAL POLICY

8

A General Overview of the Role of Accounting Services

As has been suggested earlier (Chapter 1), accountants have always stood ready to adjust their practices and procedures to accommodate changing human conditions and needs. It has been this willingness to adapt or to keep pace with economic and business conditions and to encompass the needs of decision makers in their own planning processes that has given them a very real role in the processes of development and change. Of course it is this role that has attracted the attention of the present investigators. It seems very clear that services provided by the large accounting firms in the international economy are facilitating the functioning of that economy, its growth, and its development, and aiding in the continuing strength or importance of its constituent parts.

The roots of this relationship (if not its symbiotics) are evident in economic history. Beginning with simple recording methods, accounting has developed and expanded over the centuries to encompass worldwide sets of accounts. At the outset, the development of accounting was rather slow; its methods perhaps rudimentary. These no doubt reflected both the scale and the pace of economic activity. It was not until the fourteenth century that double-entry bookkeeping came into vogue. However, elementary accounting knowledge was employed as far back as 2800 B.C. in Crete for tax and inventory purposes (Samuels and Piper, 1985, 15–16). The utility of accounting became evident to government authorities in Athens in the fifth and fourth centuries B.C. where methods were devised by them to facilitate the planning, control, and continuing assessment of activity (Costouros, 1979).

Despite such earlier forays into the recording and use of financial and economic information, conditions were not propitious for the emergence of capital and thus double-entry bookkeeping. Eventually the emergence of mercantile organizations in northern Italy signalled the need for more complete systems of accounting. The need was especially critical due to the international nature of business at the time. With the emergence of the age of exploration and empire building and the development of the great chartered companies, accounting needs expanded apace. Indeed as such needs were coming into broader demand, their sophistication was deepening as well. Clearly accounting services as facilitators in the international economy are hardly a recent phenomena. It is surprising that their role as an international adhesive has not been afforded more space by historians and others concerned with the emergence of international capitalism.

No other series of events has contributed as much collectively to the development of the free enterprise system on a world scale as did the Industrial Revolution. With the onset of that revolution in the latter half of the eighteenth century, the pace of accounting development accelerated. As mentioned in Chapter 1, mass production and advances in technology made possible and necessary a quantum increase in the scale of business. New accounting techniques emerged from the need to deal with overhead costs and vastly expanded inventories. Accounting records were required to distinguish between ownership and liabilities and between earned and contributed capital. Failure on the part of the accounting profession to accommodate these new and more complicated needs would have had serious consequences for the expansion of business in particular and the free enterprise system in general. The positive and necessary contribution that accounting services have rendered to the historical development of the international economy should not be underestimated.

As new methods of business practice emerged, the needs of decision makers in this new, expanded economic environment called for keeping accounts for greatly increased amounts of long term fixed assets. The tracking of periodic profits and losses was also necessary as was the recording of seemingly ever-increasing credit transactions. Written records and documents were increasing in importance and with them the audit function became more necessary. During the second half of the nineteenth century, the auditing of limited liability companies extended the scope of services offered by public accountants.

Aside from the expanding need for accounting services as facilitators of business, a new set of needs began to emerge in the economy of the United States during the present century. These needs were largely by-products of taxation. Suddenly many businesses and individuals found it necessary to keep more careful or complete records of income. Such an expansion of record keeping has had an understandable impact on the accounting profession. Federal securities legislation resulting from the stock market debacle of 1929 also increased the demand for accounting services.

While the demand for tax and auditing services increased, the market for management advisory services expanded as well. Accountants, because of the familiarity with the organizations they service, have been in a strong position to expand their advisory offerings. Because most large corporations assumed an international emphasis during the second half of the twentieth century, it was only natural that accounting firms should internationalize their service offerings. The firms found themselves preparing worldwide accounting records and reports. Once again the performance of such services provided the firms with the expertise to offer a wide variety of advisory services in the international sphere in much the same way as they had nurtured the domestic markets for such services in advanced economies. The expansion of the firms in the international sphere seemed both natural and necessary. Audit service for large international companies required a large professional organization with skilled, knowledgeable people acting in an independent and ethical manner with geographically disparate but centrally controlled facilities. In short, the emergence of a world economy accelerated the development of international accounting firms. As early as 1961, "a great upsurge in the number of nation-wide and world-wide audits" was reported (Penney, 1961). The nature of the international business climate has generated accounting firms of substantially increasing size. Firms from the United States and Great Britain have geared their reports to the needs of internationally dispersed holders of securities. The firms themselves have exercised substantial control over rules and procedures governing financial accounting, auditing, and reporting, individual governments notwithstanding. Thus the former have become truly international service organizations with loyalties to their purpose and, of course, to their client base. It hardly should be surprising if such large firms impact the international economy in a substantial manner through their day-to-day operations. Such impacts will undoubtedly increase as firms become fewer and larger.

As has been pointed out in Chapter 2, accounting services have grown in response to information needs focused primarily within individual nations. Standards for such services as auditing and financial reporting have tended to be set by individual nations in keeping with what they have perceived their needs to be. Perceptions and the resulting accounting are influenced by social, cultural, political, and economic considerations specific to individual nations.

Against this backdrop business enterprises have emerged in the international economy with a global perspective, as opposed to the earlier focus of business activity, which tended to be centered in specific jurisdictions. What nations are facing is an emerging "borderless world" (Ohmae, 1990) with interlinked economies. The strength of the international economy is making serious incursions into the economic sovereignty of nation states. Ohmae suggests that traditional national borders have all but disappeared (X). In this new world environment it seems clear that accounting services will have to continue to adapt in order to meet the widening needs of the business community. Within nations, the direction of changes in accounting practices depends upon internal economic adjustments and upon the strength and character of outside influences (Samuels and Piper, 1985, 30).

International direct investment has increased substantially and with it the need for new and expanded accounting services has also increased. Global financial markets have expanded to keep pace with the needs of the investment community and other international business interests. As quoted in Chapter 2, "the unending flow of money greases the machinery of the international financial markets as never before. It enables borrowers to find funds and lenders to seek the best returns for their assets" (Sesit, Monroe, and Truell, 1986, 29D). Financial markets and their operations are changing so rapidly that concerns are arising as to whether participating financial institutions and national regulators can manage them.

The international markets alluded to were facilitated by advances in communications infrastructure, floating exchange rates, the removal of currency controls, and the deregulation of transborder capital flows. Indeed, capital flows (cash movements) have become so large that it seems hardly possible for national authorities to control them. Further reductions in domestic control are evident in equity trading where global expansion has signalled the by-passing of organized stock exchanges. In that regard, the traditional idea of a national trading floor has become redundant (*Euromoney*, 1986, 43).

In the face of such sweeping changes in global business and financial markets, accounting and auditing standards remain governed largely by national jurisdictions, with major differences in reporting practices and resulting company financial statements still in evidence from country to country. Various regional and world organizations have been moving towards the harmonization of differing national standards, but the results of such initiatives by and large remain to be seen.

Regulatory practices vary from country to country. Some jurisdictions allow private professional organizations to set standards that are then overseen by a national agency. Other countries establish standards by law or indirectly through governmental bodies. Still other nations gear their standards to taxation, central planning, or other public objectives. Approaches employing a mixture of these practices are also in existence. Indeed there are wide variations in how accounting standards are set from country to country. As indicated in Chapter 2, "the social political, and economic environments specific to individual nations can explain differences in standard setting processes" (Blum and Naciri, 1989, 92).

It has been suggested that environmental characteristics, including educational, sociological, economic, political, and legal factors, underlie differences in accounting systems between nations (Arpan and Radebaugh, 1985, 24). Such characteristics become constraints on operating efficiency, explain how business firms in specific countries operate, and may even permit observers to predict actions by the firms in specific circumstances (13). Arpan and Radebaugh feel that accounting standards and practice in a specific jurisdiction should be "judged in terms of its own cultural context, and not from that of an outsider" (15). Whether their recommendation makes practical sense may depend upon how outside judges may impact the success of the total economy should they find accounting procedures in that economy less than acceptable. It is well and good in theory to make generous allowances for the real or felt needs of local circumstances in judging accounting standards, but that level of understanding by itself will not insure a successful role for the nation concerned in the world economy.

Faced with a broad array of standards, it was inevitable that the emergence of an ever more formidably linked or interdependent international economy would bring with it attempts to classify and group nations according to the standards that they employed. The role of accounting services in that international economy suggests a need for both public and private players to be able to comprehend and deal with confidence with the accounting profession in a myriad of separate jurisdictions. The specifics of attempts to classify or group countries according to their accounting standards that have been discussed in Chapter 2 need not be revived here. However, one issue suggesting the need for classification is worth repeating. The issue was highlighted in 1977 by investigators assessing the probability that financial statement information "prepared for use in a foreign country and reported upon by a reputable local (as opposed to international) accounting firm" would be viewed as presented fairly by readers in the United States (Watt,

Hammer, and Burge, 1977, 186–87). The message from that line of attack seems obvious. Foreign business interests, whether housed in the United States or elsewhere, must be able to view with some confidence financial information concerning matters internal to nations where they have real or potential interests. Failure in that regard can only lead to economic difficulties in the nations concerned.

Many elements affect financial accounting development in specific nations. Included are such things as the relation between business organizations and capital suppliers, political and economic ties with other countries, legal systems, inflation, the size and complexity of business enterprises, the sophistication of management and the financial community, and general levels of education (Mueller, Gernon, and Meek, 1991, 11–19). The orientation of accounting services in specific countries will be conditioned by the applicability of above factors.

Despite ongoing attempts to group countries according to the importance of those or other factors, it was suggested in Chapter 2 that "fundamental differences in national accounting principles, as gleaned from the reporting practices of the world's leading industrial companies, aren't that great" (Choi and Bavishi, 1983, 68). Choi and Bavishi suggested that "major differences appear to revolve around such issues as consolidation and accounting for goodwill, deferred taxes, long term leases, discretionary reserves, inflation and foreign exchange gains and losses" (68).

Auditing standards also differ internationally. The audit function is important as an independent verification when economic resources are owned by one set of individuals and controlled by another set or when public interests are at stake. The regulation of auditing and financial reporting is country specific and ranges from impressive standards in some cases to all but lacking standards in others.

Because environments differ between nations, it is conceivable that variations in accounting standards adequately reflect economic transactions and fulfill the need for information in specific environments. Unfortunately what is acceptable domestically may result in a lack of comparability from country to country, creating the potential for difficulties in the international economy. Clearly the needs of many decision makers, in particular those involved in multinational firms, transcend national boundaries. The ongoing expansion of international business transactions has generated a need for the harmonization of accounting standards in order to facilitate the availability of comparable information across international borders.

To some, the task of reducing differences among national standards has been seen as a process of standardization versus one of harmonization. As quoted earlier (Chapter 2), "standardization seeks to *eliminate* such differences by developing uniform standards, whereas harmonization seeks to *lessen* but not eliminate the differences and to make differences more reconcilable with each other" (Arpan and Radebaugh, 1985, 344). Speaking of uniformity, Holtzblatt and Fox (1983, 43) refer to a situation in which all nations would be governed by a common set of accounting standards. This they saw as rigid and inflexible, allowing for little judgment by accountants. Uniformity could also mean a single body of rules governing accounting practice throughout the world, making them similar to accounting principles in the United States (43). They saw harmonization as allowing for the continuing retention of national standards by nations which cooperate in reducing friction (44). This last approach would appear to be more practical or achievable than standardization.

In search of some degree of harmony and standardization, various regional organizations have emerged. Some groups are formed with governmental representatives and appear to be rather political. Others are private and voluntary. The UN has been involved in efforts to set international accounting standards since the 1970s. The UN International Working Group of Exports on International Standards of Accounting and Reporting developed minimum disclosures to be made by multinational corporations (MNCs) to national governments. Material covered went well beyond accounting to include matters of social responsibility, labor relations policies, employment breakdowns, environmental effects, and the disclosure of transfer pricing policy. In some circles, UN initiatives are seen as designed to protect developing nations from multinational business interests. Of course the UN possesses no power to legislate, but rather must rely upon persuasion. Even this power is limited in practice, and the Western Industrial Group has sought to discourage UN efforts on the grounds that the UN was not the appropriate group to set standards (Arpan and Radebaugh, 1985, 348). Thus UN efforts have been polarized politically between developed and developing nations and, as a consequence, have little chance of reconciliation or agreement (348).

Efforts at harmonization have been ongoing within the European Economic Community. Member countries have been given several years to adjust their laws to comply with approved directives. However, the directives have not been considered as laws and in any case only establish minimum requirements. Despite their seemingly weak power to impact individual nations, they are viewed by some as hindrances to efforts at global harmonization.

Despite very mixed signals emanating from advanced nations with respect to the harmonization or standardization of accounting standards, the development of worldwide standards for the presentation of financial statements is a major goal of the International Accounting Standards Committee (IASC). As quoted earlier (Chapter 2), that organization has been seeking "a basis for underdeveloped countries to follow as an accounting profession emerged in those countries" (Wyatt, 1989, 106). Beyond that, it has wanted to increase the "focus on accounting and reporting responsibilities of multinational companies" (106). According to Wyatt, standards emanating from the IASC have been developed in broad terms often offering two or more alternatives. He saw little impact from them in the United States and suggested that they represented little more than a curiosity (105).

Despite this view, considerable interest has been shown in the IASC standards on the part of the international business community. As reported earlier (Chapter 2) "The *Journal of Accountancy* (1990) reported that in a Touche Ross International survey of 278 major multinational companies from 12 countries, two-thirds . . . indicated that they comply substantially with IASC standards." Some of the firms indicated that reducing alternatives would improve the quality of information and thus make data more usable (see Chapter 2). Beyond this seeming support of the IASC standards on the part of various multinational firms, the International Federation of Accountants (IFAC) recognizes the standard-setting authority of the IASC. For its part, the IFAC seeks "to develop and enhance a coordinated worldwide accountancy profession with harmonized standards" (Chandler, 1990). Thus there seems to be substantial support for international accounting standards that are at least harmonized.

There is no doubt that harmonization would be of assistance to all of the players in the international economy. Firms operating in that economy encounter complex accounting problems that are foreign to domestic operations. Multinational corporations must cope with variations in accounting standards and currencies, legal systems, and cultural considerations. They must deal with corporate accounting and reporting on a global basis. Their reporting must be designed for decision making at their headquarters as well as within local units. Their planning and control functions, including transfer pricing, must adapt to a wider diversity. Performance evaluations must consider many different local environmental factors. Using global information and communications systems, the firms must expand their internal control, audit, and management accounting operations.

Reporting, most particularly to interests external to the corporation, is frequently global in scope, requiring various accounting consolidations with their compliment of complexities. Consolidated reports frequently mask or obscure important information concerning geographical regions, product lines, and other major components of the overall business. To facilitate decision making, segmental reporting or disaggregation must accompany consolidations. Of course, accounting in specific jurisdictions must be adequate for local needs. To facilitate consolidation, global accounting records must be transformed into a common format. Such a format may be that of the home base of the corporation or it may be that of the country supplying capital or credit. In cases where local accounting standards are employed, all reports must be adjusted to achieve consistency with the accounting standards of the home country or the reporting country.

In some cases, multinational firms produce financial reports employing several national bases. This is in keeping with the needs and realities of raising capital from many jurisdictions, a practice that inevitably expands the need for various types of disclosures. As emphasized in Chapter 3, "differences in disclosure levels among nations are rapidly narrowing, and . . . increased disclosure can lead to lower costs of capital for business enterprises" (Mueller, Gernon, and Meek, 1991, 65). More and more, the multinationals are preparing financial statements using IASC standards. Firms may be at a disadvantage by not following some type of internationally acceptable financial reporting that may go beyond local needs (5). It goes without saying that the analysis of reports must factor in variations in financial and business practices under which the operations occurred.

Beyond the considerations alluded to here is the problem of changing currency conversion rates between countries, which result in some measure from international variations in the level of inflation. Various nations have attempted to deal with inflation in accounting reports (AlHashim and Arpan, 1988, 109). However, as inflation subsides, such jurisdictions typically revert to the historical cost standard (109). The lack of objective evidence of either general or specific price change measurement appears to be the fundamental problem with price level accounting.

Changes in the exchange rates between currencies regardless of cause can impact cross-currency transactions and thus the translation of cross-currency financial statements. The method of accounting for gains, losses, and currency translation differences can impact the portrayal of operating results and financial position. Several factors affect the need for the currency translation of intracompany reports. In cases where the home office exerts tight planning and control of cross-border branches or subsidiaries, it will frequently require all reports in its currency. This will not negate the need for reverse translation on the part of branch operations where business is conducted in local currency. Even where subsidiaries are more independent, they will undoubtedly need to provide translated financial reports for their parent organization. As indicated earlier (Chapter 3), "accounting information requirements of a parent company should generally not be allowed to overshadow local accounting information requirements. In effect, two distinct sets of information requirements exist and they require translation and reconciliation back and forth" (Choi and Mueller, 1984, 111).

Selecting the appropriate currency exchange rate is an accounting dilemma. Because currency conversion rates change over time, one might use either the current rate or historical rates in the assumed currency conversions when translating foreign statements to a reporting currency. Gains or losses through the exchange of currency become a part of transaction results as conversions occur. The party who must convert to a local currency assumes the risk of changes in the exchange rate and the resulting gain or loss.

Fundamental differences between transactions and translations exist and should be noted. Accounting for transactions includes actual currency conversions, and the risks of changing rates must be born by one party or another. Translation as mentioned earlier (Chapter 3) results in the expression of financial reports at a point in time in the currency of a country in which the transaction did not take place and where currency conversions did not occur. Translation facilitates information availability by providing it in terms of a single reporting currency, regardless of what currency or currencies actually were used in the transactions at issue.

The fact that exchange rates are subject to continuous change is a major problem inherent in cross-border transactions. It can cause sizable unrealized gains or losses from transactions or translations. When rates change directions, reported earnings are impacted. It appears realistic to include unrealized but anticipated income adjustments even though conversion rates are subject to change. Foreign business units involved in multiyear transactions must take notice of this.

Foreign subsidiaries operating in particular nations on long-term bases may have their cash flows in local currencies. This is especially probable where business is conducted largely within host nations, with few transactions with parent companies. In such cases, it makes little sense to view the units involved as doing business in currencies other than those of their host nations.

Inflation impacts both planning and actual operations globally and locally. In many cases, it may divert the attention of managers and prove detrimental to normal activities. As quoted earlier (Chapter 3), "differing rates of inflation mean that real costs of production and other factors change dynamically relative to one another so that a global system must be continuously cost balanced" (Scott, 1978, 1212). Changes in relative costs may shift production and resources between countries (1212).

Planning and control are dependent upon the national environment within which firms operate. Variations between those environments further complicate international planning and control. Governmental controls and taxes vary between jurisdictions as do business practices, customs, and conditions. Planning and control frequently require personal interactions in addition to written communications. Of course relationships on both levels become more complex when national borders are involved. Cross-border communications systems may be incompatible or may involve variations in expertise. Managers in various jurisdictions may exhibit many of the same attitudinal problems that domestic managers have in dealing with matters of budgeting and control.

Managers "may have too little empathy for cultures other than their own" (Scott, 1978, 1211). They may prefer independence over collaboration and, beyond that, may be resistant to change. As the number of nations involved increases, so do these problems. Things that are possible in certain nations may be less so in others. Although environmental factors tend to change slowly within nations, the pace of such adjustments may differ from one jurisdiction to another. Such variations may throw off segments of the plans devised by multinational firms (1211).

Although corporations have been carrying out planning, control, and evaluation functions for some time, there are those who suggest that "the development of comprehensive MNC international planning and control systems with long range strategic focus is next" (Mueller, Gernon, and Meek, 1991, 104). Variations in planning, controlling, and evaluating with respect to domestic and foreign operations relate to the complexities of differing environmental considerations that may create obstacles to uniform corporate reporting on a global scale (108).

As Mueller, Gernon, and Meek recognize, requiring uniformity can hardly be expected to make such barriers disappear (1991, 108). In certain Third World jurisdictions, adequate accounting may not be generally or easily available. Multinationals operating in such jurisdictions need consistent accounting and reports if they are to compare those reports and evaluations. It has been suggested that multinationals should require reports from their operating units in terms of home country standards (Mueller, Gernon, and Meek, 1991, 108). Those authors recognize that accounting and reporting systems must be flexible enough to meet the needs of both home offices and subsidiaries. Such needs notwithstanding, adaptability and uniformity can be at cross purposes (108).

Planning and control functions for corporations can take various forms. Scott has distinguished between multinational holding companies (MHCs) and multinational enterprises (MEs) (1978, 1213). The latter are referred to by some as MNCs. MHCs use foreign subsidiaries to manufacture and sell products within specific foreign countries with little interaction between other foreign locations or the parent company. Such subsidiaries may well have local autonomy for operations that can be considered to be investment centers for accounting and evaluation purposes. They may have limited intercourse with a parent from which they may receive investment funds and to which profits may be returned.

MNCs by contrast are coordinated on a global basis with an eye to maximizing returns on investments. Companies may move from multinational holding company status toward that of the multinational corporations. In the process, all of their operations tend to become "integrated vertically and horizontally . . . to the extent that this is possible within the constraints imposed by national governments' policies and the limitations of managerial and information systems technology (Scott, 1978, 1214). Of course, local managers are best able to respond to local needs while headquarter managers have an advantage in understanding and responding to global needs and concerns.

In MHCs, long-range planning and capital budgeting tend to concentrate on the local host country. The parent firm aggregates the planning for the various operations into a corporate plan. It appears as though firms that are able to move towards global integration secure substantial competitive advantages by so doing. Planning and control on a global scale are needed if firms are to enjoy flexible adaptation to changing conditions. As Scott has warned, "the company that simply utilizes its domestic control systems abroad . . . will experience grave control problems in its international systems" (1978, 1221). If their international operations are to be well meshed, firms require workable global evaluation systems. Such arrangements provide for rational resource allocations and early warnings where operations are going astray, and they form a basis for reviewing the performance of managers and giving them motivation (Shapiro, 1978, 454).

In the case of MNCs, performance evaluation systems based upon profit or investment centers seem appropriate in some situations, but appear to be less so in the case of local managers, since such individuals lack the responsibility for many procedures. Budgets may be an effective evaluation tool for both MHCs and MNCs in some cases. There may be problems associated with treating foreign units as profit or investment centers due to the ways in which transfer prices are employed by MNCs. Although such prices between domestic units are generally established on an equitable basis, the same can hardly be said in the case of international operations.

In that theater, transfer pricing serves various corporate goals. In some jurisdictions, it can be used in the avoidance of taxation. It is also helpful in cash transfers between nations. Clearly, transfer pricing can be at cross purposes to the goals and objectives of governments. The general objectives of transfer pricing were highlighted earlier in this volume (Chapter 3). Briefly, they include the minimization of worldwide income taxes and import duties, the avoidance of financial restrictions, the managing of currency fluctuations, and the winning of host country approval (Mueller, Gernon, and Meek, 1991, 128).

It is clear that transfer pricing impacts corporate operations in Third World locations. The host nations may influence corporate operations where transfer pricing is perceived to impact their interests. Such influences may take the form of profit repatriation restrictions, exchange controls, joint venture constraints, tariffs and customs duties, and income tax liability (Kim and Miller, 1984). Despite such obvious obstacles that governments can create, "the advantages of transfer price manipulation remain considerable, given the market imperfections of today's international business environment" (Nobes and Parker, 1988, 175).

Using transfer pricing in the search for profit maximization and risk reduction is at best complex. If such pricing does not reflect arm's-length prices, economic efficiency may be impaired. Such pricing policies can conflict with the traditional goals of profit center motivation and accountability. Transfer pricing practices can have severe impacts on the Third World. In poorer nations, tax rates are often higher and import duties on manufacturing inputs are relatively low. The threat of transfer pricing creates a dilemma for developing countries in that they must conform to developed world standards (Lall, 1973, 416).

Since 1976, multinational firms headquartered in the United States have been required to supply segment information that includes in-house (inter-unit) sales or transfers between geographical areas. This segment information must show transfers on the basis of the price actually used.

The provision of such data has been facilitated by improved accounting information systems. External reporting in an accounting context usually includes annual financial statements, tax returns, and other required government reports, all of which must be prepared in keeping with the needs or requirements of external users. Even internal reporting tends to be set up to conform to the needs of its external counterpart.

Whatever accounting information system a corporation adopts, it should be compatible with organizational structure and designed to supply needed information to all levels of decision making. Domestic systems are made to be consistent with home country environmental factors. "Exporting such a system ignores the foreign subsidiaries' operating environment and may result in a breakdown of communication" (Mueller, Gernon, and Meek, 1991, 98). It seems to be clear that the scale, geographical spread, and diversity of the data that must be dealt with by multinational firms requires accounting on a global basis. Indeed, as quoted earlier (Chapter 3), "International business is turning management accounting into a global profession, unrestricted by national boundaries" (Langdon, 1986, 58). Thus accounting procedures within corporations are assuming international dimensions that are at least as broad as those that the international accounting firms have embraced.

9

The Services, the International Economy, and the Third World

The expansion of accounting services in the second half of the twentieth century is in keeping with the ascendancy of service activities to prominence in various economies throughout the world. Economists have come to regard service expansion as a logical consequence of the growth process. Some have seen it as a result of rising incomes while others have cited the expansion of urban populations as its cause (see McKee, 1988).

Despite the historical accuracy of the causes cited, it would appear that the continuing service expansion requires a somewhat more complex appraisal. In Chapter 5, services were represented as "a way of doing business in relation to the activities of either firms or households" that "grows more rapidly because it pays to do business in new ways as the economy develops" (Castle and Findley, 1988, 5). Others have seen the share of employment held by services as "partly a function of structural changes in the 'environment' which can be interpreted as reflecting the development of the economy over time" (Stern and Hockman, 1988, 34). In addition to urbanization, they saw a changing employment situation for women as instrumental in the conditions that they were describing. They suggested that increasingly specialized service organizations are emerging as particular service functions are divorcing themselves from both firms and households. They also spoke of technological change as an unbundler of services from goods. Beyond the phenomena cited here, they saw causes of rising service employment in the increasing availability of part-time service jobs, the welfare state, and also "the increasing importance of international trade and investment" (34). This last phenomenon has undoubtedly been a factor in the expansion of accounting services.

Although few would dispute the increasing importance of services internationally, Michael Porter has suggested that the relative importance of international service success to specific nations versus the record in manufacturing is still being debated (1990, 266). In any such debate, it must be remembered that services do provide linkages in manufacturing chains that, in turn, add both jobs and stability to national economies (McKee, 1988, 23). Service activities "generally maintain the flexibility to shift to accommodate the needs of new industrial sectors" (23). In this way, services are involved in growth processes in a positive fashion and may also be diluting the effects of industrial decline. It seems hardly surprising that services are extending their roles in both the operation and the expansion of modern economies to the international sphere. Indeed, as suggested earlier (Chapter 4), the world economy as it exists today would not have developed without much growth and continuing improvement in various service subsectors over the past 20 years.

Today services cannot be regarded as mere facilitators in the international economy. They are actually being traded in that economy and in many instances have become internationalized in their own right. As Porter suggests (1990, 266), firms in that position can easily adapt their offerings to local markets, thus maintaining a competitive edge over potential competitors in host jurisdictions. He sees economies-of-scale in international service firms allowing them to "spread the costs of technology development, training infrastructure, and other activities over worldwide sales revenues" (251). Because of the strength of international service firms, their role in the international economy, and their impacts in domestic economies, hosting them should be carefully assessed.

In particular Third World locations, it may be that certain service firms will position themselves as dictated by the competitive needs of the firms in question as they pursue the goal of satisfying their customers who may themselves be multinational firms. The positioning of specific business services in Third World settings depends upon the external linkages enjoyed by the economies in question rather than on what those linkages may be presumed to be in the future. The services in question can hardly be presumed to emerge in keeping with the domestic needs of host countries, and policies that might be employed to encourage their emergence are by no means obvious.

It seems probable that the international expansion of various business-related services is fueled by the needs of large manufacturing corporations (Noyelle and Dutka, 1988, 29). Noyelle and Dutka suggested that U.S.-based service firms moving into foreign jurisdictions often found that local firms had little expertise and thus "U.S. firms played a key role in many countries in creating a domestic market" (29). If this is the case, foreign firms may have a good deal to do with the structure and perhaps the expansion of the economies concerned. If this is true, impacts may be difficult to quantify. As mentioned earlier, the internationalized services of international business units may preclude the development of domestic service groups, resulting in unmeasurable influences upon the economies concerned (Chapter 4).

Adding to the difficulty of assessing service impacts in host jurisdictions is the need to distinguish between trade and foreign direct investment. Since services can be difficult to transport, the on-site presence of suppliers may be indicated (United Nations, 1987, 23). Whether this means access to national distribution systems or that foreign suppliers have the right to sign distribution contracts, there is little doubt that such arrangements will impact host countries significantly (23). It would seem that such impacts would be more noticeable in smaller and developing economies. They would vary in significance depending upon whether or not the services are geared to the domestic economy or to international interests.

Some locations may enjoy an exposure to specific business services when they are positioned to meet the needs of the production units of multinational firms. If such facilitators are positioned to produce for domestic markets, the impact of the services that they generate may be considerable. If the service groups themselves are international in scope, their operations may bear a foreign operating mode, which may have considerable impact upon shaping local business services and, beyond that, perhaps the local economy.

The service sector has been attracting "a significant and increasing share of the flows of the foreign direct investment in the world economy" (United Nations, 1987, 60). The report found such flows to Third World nations to be noticeable but less significant than those between developed economies. It is important to note that the report saw factors influencing the decision to invest in services as asserting significant impacts upon both the size and the direction of foreign investment flows (60). The significance of this can hardly be lost upon those concerned with the direction of development in Third World economies.

It seems tautological to suggest that various services are indispensable to nations wishing to increase or even maintain their levels of participation in the international economy. Policy commitments related to such goals may alter domestic economies irrevocably (McKee, 1991). In some nations where the availability of sophisticated cadres of business services is limited, developmental processes may be affected adversely (United Nations, 1987, 61). There may be Third World economies that do not enjoy the option of accepting or rejecting the location of various international business services. Such services as facilitators of international business may not be needed in certain locations. Profit-seeking services should be presumed to limit as best they can the location of their facilities in the international economy to positions presumed to be profitable. Nonetheless, advances in transportation and communications have broadened the menu of potential locations. With expanded options available for the location of industrial units comes more options with respect to the location of facilitating business services.

It seems clear that Third World nations with opportunities for stronger international linkages will be hard pressed to turn them down. Accepting the linkages will no doubt encourage a continuing infusion of investment in international services that, in turn, will tend to further strengthen the linkages. Undoubtedly the price of development is becoming stronger international linkages and, with them, having less domestic control of economies. As unpalatable as this option may appear to some, it may be the only road to development and is undoubtedly a road that was largely unavailable until the relatively recent emergence of a sophisticated international service sector.

Accounting has never been a strictly national phenomenon since its techniques and its impacts have cut through national boundaries in directions dictated by commerce and political influence (Hopwood, 1989, 9). International accounting services have expanded in tune with the demands of international business. Through their expansion, they have influenced the direction of the international economy and its constituent parts, whether territorial or economic.

The accounting firms themselves have been showing more interest in the international aspects of their dealings (Hopwood, 1989, 1). Indeed, it seems that international considerations are impinging on accounting procedures in advanced economies. It was suggested in Chapter 5 that as accounting emerges on the stage of an increasingly integrated and perhaps standardized world economy, more and more inroads will undoubtedly be made into traditional ways of performing accounting functions in individual countries. Accountants are aware of the importance of cultural differences in the setting of accounting standards (Bloom and Naciri, 1989) and, indeed, that the impact of culture on accounting must be considered (Perera, 1989). They are also aware that certain international accounting standards may be inappropriate in Third World jurisdictions (Hoye, 1989).

These issues present problems for accountants and economists alike. Practices that seem essential to a reasonable functioning of the world economy may not seem reasonable at all in certain jurisdictions. In such settings, if they are rejected or abridged, they may block economic progress itself. The dilemma for various Third World nations is clear. Resistance may stifle development while acceptance may exact a grim toll in valued traditions and cultural identity.

Of course, standardization can be both good and bad. Internationally, it can generate economies-of-scale and resultant cost reductions with greater profit potential. With it, personnel and procedures become interchangeable, leading to much more flexibility. This, in turn, shortens the response time needed to add or subtract with respect to operations in specific areas as needs change. Clients can rely upon a more homogeneous and thus predictable quality of service in various locations. Because this is so, competition between firms for clients may be heightened in the international sphere. Despite this, the firms in question may find themselves with far less scope for differentiating their products as clients search for acceptable levels of international service uniformity. There is little question that clients have real leverage over the nature of the services provided. In such a climate, it is hardly surprising that the firms have been developing new product lines and new territorial markets. Through these ends, they increase their potential for acquiring new clients for their auditing services.

On the negative side, standardization creates inflexibilities that can impact both client and host jurisdictions. Clients may find that they are having to adjust to the procedures of the international accounting firms. The firms themselves may absorb local firms or, under other circumstances, drive them out of business.

Despite certain drawbacks, the confidence instilled by the presence of standardized accounting procedures can stimulate both domestic and international business pursuits, a circumstance particularly attractive to Third World jurisdictions. In effect, the firms may instill improved business confidence that, in turn, contributes to expansion and thus to the processes of growth and development.

As suggested earlier (Chapter 5), "new business practices, changes in the financial and economic environment, and new levels of accountability" generate accounting change (Cook, 1989, 34). Cook was of the opinion that financial innovations are often responses to taxes or restrictions imposed by governments. In the international arena, they are designed to assist businesses in dealing with such taxes and restrictions. If the accounting firms are providers of such innovations, they are becoming facilitators in the manner attributed to business services in general (McKee, 1988). As such they may be rendering various attempts at international regulation less effective and thus may be contributing further to the strength and efficiency of the international economy.

The provision of accounting services in the world economy has become more and more the preserve of large firms. Concentration in the accounting industry is increasing in the Third World as well. It may appear that there is a role for smaller accounting firms in the Third World, but the reality seems to be that the advent of the large international competitors tends to absorb or eliminate smaller competitors. In an increasingly concentrated industry, the importance of such concentration and internationalization "is matched by the increased diversity of accounting services" and the willingness of large firms to launch any service capable of earning fees (Daniels, Leyshon, and Thrift, 1988, 324). An increased emphasis on various consulting services is making the accounting firms more important players internationally. It would appear that nations and other jurisdictions within the world economy would be well advised to improve their understanding of the impacts of such firms. This is nowhere more important than in Third World economies.

Without the level of economic integration that is now evident in the world economy, it seems unlikely that the accounting firms could have become major international players. In the same vein, their roles in Third World economies might have been slower to develop. The level of integration that is apparent is attributable in large measure to improvements in transportation and communications. Despite their own dependence upon improved international economic integration, the accounting firms themselves supply services to both manufacturing concerns and other service firms. It is becoming clear that the accounting firms are central among the groupings of service facilitators. Their traditional audit functions contribute to an order in the economies where they are supplied.

There is little doubt that the basic services of international accounting firms can have strong impacts with respect to the strengthening of Third World economies. If those basic accounting services can improve the operating efficiency of such economies, the new consulting services if anything should be expected to strengthen already positive impacts. The ever-increasing menu of consulting services being offered may be provided to governmental agencies as well as to the private sector.

Accounting firms have been entering new jurisdictions as their potential for profit becomes clear. However, beyond the prospect of direct profitability lies the necessity of retaining established international business accounts. As their clients move into new locations, the accounting firms have a choice between expanding their own operations or risking the loss of clients to competitors that do. It seems clear that many expansion decisions are dictated by the need felt by the firms to retain their international competitive positions. Their expansionary pressure reinforces the normal business desire to extend markets.

For Third World economies, the advent of the accounting firms appears to signal better linkages to the international economy. Such linkages in turn may stimulate economic activity and thus development prospects. The consulting services provided may aid in positioning multinational business facilities and may also be utilized advantageously by domestic firms. It may be that such impacts may be especially helpful in economies that are both small and poor. Even among multinationals with no direct contact with the accounting firms, indirect impacts may materialize in cases where the activities of the accounting firms impact Third World economies such that they become more attractive to those multinationals.

The addition of various consulting services to the offerings of the accounting firms signals an obvious enlargement of their role as facilitators. There appears to be no shortage of clients for such services in the international economy. As the firms supply the needs of these clients, they are also furthering international economic integration. Their actions may well impact diverse components of that economy and may not be limited to their own clients.

In cases where governmental agencies are major clients for various services offered by the firms, those services may play major roles with respect to development. The extent to which this is happening can be seen in examples cited in Chapter 6. Obviously the impacts of any foreign consultants hired by governmental agencies should reflect the needs perceived by the government concerned. If the consultants are hired to pursue the interests of international businesses with interests in particular jurisdictions, they will have greater scope for generating impacts that are poorly meshed with the developmental needs of the nations concerned. It would appear that the consulting activities of the large accounting firms may well encompass practically any aspect of business or economic activity on a worldwide basis.

From the point of view of particular jurisdictions, where the services of the firms are increasing the involvement or possible integration of those jurisdictions with the world economy, various positive overspills may occur. For example, when a Third World economy becomes better integrated with the world at large, foreign exchange may be easier to obtain, more employment opportunities may become available in the domestic economy, and that economy itself may experience a greater impetus toward growth and development. Of course, such developments may bring with them an erosion of economic sovereignty as the economies in question become more obvious components of the world economy.

For those concerned with the direction of impacted economies, the situation requires an assessment of their priorities. The costs and benefits of what is occurring must be assessed on a case-by-case basis. Even in this regard, the accounting firms may have expertise to offer. By doing so they may facilitate the development plans of the jurisdictions concerned. It seems apparent that Third World governmental agencies can hardly ignore the potential of what the firms may have available. The firms themselves must carry an awareness of the potential developmental impact of what they are doing. Indeed, it would appear that both the firms and host governments will be best served if sound development practices and growth patterns are stimulated.

It seems evident that the accounting firms, by servicing their clients, are impacting the movement and positioning of both financial and physical capital. Hence, they are also influencing the differential strengths of various locations in the world economy. Various services that accounting firms supply to independent businesses exert both stabilizing and supportive influences on Third World jurisdictions. In the absence of the major accounting firms, various business services may be in very short supply in Third World nations. As such services become more readily available in such nations through the actions of the accounting firms, they facilitate the operations of multinational manufacturing firms and, as mentioned earlier, contribute to a more fully integrated international economy. The availability of these consulting services widens the same competitive stimulants that prompted the accounting firms to expand their basic services. Those stimulants are now assuming causal roles in the expansion of consulting activities. The need to remain competitive is directing pressure toward opening new markets and expanding service menus.

As the demand for consulting services expands, the major accounting firms, with their office networks in place, have substantial advantages over other consulting organizations seeking to expand in the international marketplace. The accounting firms may also be better positioned and equipped to supply consulting services in Third World economies than are the would-be domestic purveyors of such services where they exist. Indeed, the proven ability of the accounting firms to expand into new service lines may, for all practical purposes, preclude domestic consulting aspirants.

It seems clear that the new service lines that are continuing to develop within the large accounting firms will expand, constrained only by the needs of the economies that they service. The firms are clearly in a strong position to offer their new service lines anywhere in the world where clients can be found. What seems evident is what has been described as the "systematization and in some cases standardization of the process of delivering services" (Porter, 1990, 245). Although Porter was generalizing, his remark seems apt to describe the practice of the accounting firms. Porter spoke of organizations "capable of replicating services consistently as well as in multiple locations by using standardized facilities, operating modes, and procedures to guide employees" (28).

The accounting firms are also well positioned for the international dissemination of business information. Users of such information are undoubtedly aware that the firms from which it emanates can provide basic accounting services as well. They may also be coming to the realization that the accounting firms are equipped to assist in an ever-widening variety of operational issues in a growing selection of international locations. It seems entirely possible that the dissemination of information is not just a way for expanding service clienteles but can very well channel the operations of those clienteles to selected locations that have attractive business environments.

The accounting firms have an added advantage in offering consulting services that can be funneled through local offices. At the very least, local offices can serve as contact or liaison points if the firm's specialists are to be brought in from abroad. It would appear that the actual presence of the accounting firms in numerous Third World economies facilitates the marketing of consulting services.

It is quite possible for consulting activities to emanate from the offices of the accounting firms in Third World jurisdictions hardly noted as manufacturing sites. Sophisticated service groupings do emerge in such locations. Offshore banking centers are a prime example, as are other nonmanufacturing economies that seem able to market selections of services internationally or perhaps regionally. From such settings, the consulting services offered by the accounting firms become facilitators with respect to the operation of the international economy. As such they expedite economic relations (business) between advanced nations as well as between those nations and various Third World economies. They contribute to the integration of the international economy and, of course, to its expansion and continued viability.

In the Third World, such services are clearly contributors to growth processes. By assisting local activities, offering various managerial and advisory inputs, and aiding the operation of business organizations in the world economy, they undoubtedly increase the potential for profitable business operations in Third World locations. It seems clear that they are functioning in Third World settings in a manner similar to sophisticated cadres of services operating in advanced economies. Those latter services are known to be instrumental in facilitating the operations of production as well as in cushioning economic change (McKee, 1988).

In smaller Third World nations, the consulting services emanating from accounting firms may provide assistance to nations on a regional basis. Various examples may be found in the Caribbean basin. In such instances, the firms are assisting in forms of international economic integration on a regional level. This practice presumably should improve growth potential for the regions concerned by initiating international linkages that may serve them well in relation to the world economy. Of course, services geared to business operations in the world economy, when located in smaller nations or territories, may give such locations roles in the international economy that may otherwise have been closed to them. In short, it seems clear that the services in question have much to offer nations wishing to strengthen their development potential. In smaller nations, it may well be that foreign linkages occasioned by such services may provide the only means for economic betterment. Thus services that were regarded as secondary concerns or by-products from the viewpoint of the accounting firms have become very important to the processes of development and international economic integration.

Some of the developmental options would hardly have been possible without the major advances in transportation and communications that have been occurring during the second half of the twentieth century. In consort with those changes have come the development of various sophisticated services in the world economy. Today it is feasible for multinational firms to place components of their production lines in numerous worldwide locations, the only constraints being profit potential, the nature of transportation and communications, and the availability of other services necessary to their operations.

The service infrastructure has been seen as nothing less than "a technological revolution spreading across major segments of manufacturing services" (Cohen and Zysman, 1987, 80), a revolution based upon wide applications "of new microelectronic-based products, production, and telecommunications technologies" (80). Cohen and Zysman have suggested that a new infrastructure has emerged from a convergence between computers and communications technology. In their view, the telecommunications equipment and service industries have become strategic industrial sectors, and these new telecommunications will change competitive processes on an economy-wide basis (187). Their analysis, although geared to conditions within the United States, would appear to be applicable to the international sphere, including Third World jurisdictions.

Accepting the fact that telecommunications technology together with computers have altered the industrial and business landscape is hardly grounds for ignoring the parts played by various sophisticated service subsectors in the accelerating processes of change. As alluded to earlier (Chapter 7), "by extending markets and providing more flexibility in production chains, services have dramatically altered the processes of production" (McKee, 1988, 115). Various services are strengthening international economic linkages by facilitating the movement of materials and financial assets through national boundaries.

In some cases, services have emerged to facilitate the operations of specific industries. This can be seen in service clusters that house manufacturing facilities that have emerged in various locations internationally. In such cases, it may be that services have followed manufacturing firms to accommodate the needs of the firms. In some cases, services can be seen as integral to the actual functioning of industries, even though they may have functions separate from or beyond the industries in question. The linkages between various activities are rendering previously recognizable industrial or sectoral boundaries indistinct. As Robinson (1989, 42) has suggested, the clear distinctions previously common to the marketplace have been blurred by technological change. In this type of business climate, it seems logical that the configuration of accounting services has been changing, and it should hardly be surprising to see the accounting firms moving beyond their basic offerings.

Clearly technological change has encouraged if not caused these adjustments. Robinson suggests that technological change has had profound impacts upon international business operations (1989, 43). He sees functions as easily transferable geographically and labor being replaced by information technology equipment. Certainly the accounting firms have benefitted from the types of changes being alluded to. It seems evident that improvements in the processing of information, the expanding role of computers, and the actual information networking have collectively facilitated the internationalizing of accounting operations. It seems clear that the emergence of international accounting firms and the flexibility that they have gained from technology may have dramatic impacts upon the development potential of various Third World settings.

The firms in question can easily transfer their functions from place to place, including locations in Third World jurisdictions. With the new technological infrastructure at their disposal, the firms can deliver a level of service that might have been previously beyond their means in locations where basic accounting expertise is a scarce commodity. Of course, it seems obvious that the greater locational scope that technology has afforded the accounting firms will translate into developmental impacts in the settings they select. The technology used to implant the firms in Third World locations may generate demonstration effects, whereby it is soon being applied to other pursuits. In such cases, it seems clear that the accounting firms have assumed causal roles, well beyond what the provision of efficient accounting services may indicate and certainly well beyond any employment multipliers attributable to increasingly efficient accounting services.

In spite of the linkages suggested here, the accounting firms may never have seen themselves as technological institutions per se. However, their expanding consulting menus may be moving them in that direction. Technological institutions have been defined to include those contributing in any recognizable manner to processes relating to technological innovation, whether in the promotion or financing of research, and to the development of technological capacities (Jéquier and Yao-Su Hu, 1989, 6). It certainly seems as though the accounting firms are operating within these parameters in Third World nations through both direct and indirect impacts. Speaking in terms of growth or development, the obvious scientific activities in laboratories, universities, and research centers may be less important than "the embodiment of technology in investment and production in different sectors of the economy" (86).

Certainly the accounting firms exacerbate such embodiments in certain ways by supplying standardized international services through their technological networking. By the capacity that they have for establishing themselves in various locations to meet the needs of their customers, they are assisting in the international transfer of technology, which appears to be an inevitable adjunct to the functioning of multinational firms.

It is quite evident that accounting firms can impact the dissemination of technology in Third World settings and thus influence developmental processes. It seems that they are playing an important role in the expansion of Third World economies and in the linking of those jurisdictions to the rest of the world. One of the major advantages of the accounting technology of the firms is its external linking ability. The firms may contribute to a business climate conducive to success among enterprises looking toward external markets as well as to those with more local ambitions. By supplying consulting services, they may be able to contribute to the adoption of more efficient technologies.

From time to time, arguments have been posed with respect to the Third World for the use of industrial technology below the cutting edge by international standards. The general veracity of such arguments falls beyond the parameters of the current discussion. Suffice it to say that they seem far less persuasive in the case of various sophisticated services. It has been suggested that the basic functions of know-how in the Third World have to do with the enhancement of technological capability in various spheres (Forsyth, 1990, 73). Although Forsyth was not thinking of accounting or other business services, his views can be easily adjusted to accommodate those pursuits.

The accounting firms, by encouraging systematic record keeping throughout host economies, not only facilitate business in a domestic sense, but also render the economies in question more acceptable targets for foreign business linkages. Lessons learned from the firms should continue to strengthen accounting procedures throughout host economies with the result that the economies themselves are strengthened. The accounting firms can become local training grounds for accounting talent. Simultaneously they can interact with local business interests in ways allowing them to adjust their service offerings to local markets. Thus the firms should be able to accommodate the accounting needs of the local market while simultaneously offering linkages for local business interests to the world economy. By such services, they should be able to contribute to the general strengthening of Third World host economies.

Basic accounting operations can improve business climates through diffusion. As seen earlier (Chapter 8), this is "an informal process which relates to the transfer of information either in embodied form through movement of personnel or through interaction between customers and suppliers" (Forsyth, 1990, 74). It may be too soon for a general appraisal of the impact of the international accounting firms in Third World locations, but it would appear that there are grounds for cautious optimism. Unquestionably, there are grounds for interest on the part of those concerned with development policy and economic planning in Third World settings.

10

Some Final Policy Reflections

Any attempt to access the policy options or responsibilities of national governments, with respect to the changes which developments in the nature and extent of accounting services and their delivery are initiating, must be pursued against the backdrop of the international economy. As emphasized more than once in the current volume, services are extending their roles in both the operation and the expansion of modern economies to the international sphere. In fact, the global economy owes its present format — if not its very existence — to the growth and continuing improvement of various services over the past two decades. Among the services in question, those supplied by the international accounting firms, as well as accounting functions internal to multinational corporations, occupy an important place.

There is little doubt that various services provided by large accounting firms are facilitating the functioning of the international economy and its constituent parts. In this regard, they are in partnership with various other service subsectors that facilitate business, not the least of which are those related to transportation and communications. Jurisdictions where any or all of these types of services are underrepresented or where governments actively restrict their operations can expect to suffer some disadvantage with respect to their international business and economic linkages. In advanced economies, this would translate into difficulties in maintaining their viability and strength, while in Third World jurisdictions it may mean definite roadblocks to economic expansion.

Although governments can restrict accounting and various other services, which operate internationally through rules and regulations, the services in question may also impact host economies and their governments. The international accounting firms, for example, have been exercising considerable control over both the rules and the procedures governing financial accounting, auditing, and reporting, regardless of the existence of governments. The firms in question are not aligned with the interests of specific national governments but rather, as genuinely international service organizations, they pursue their interests and those of their clients. There can be little doubt that they are having substantial impacts upon the international economy and its constituent jurisdictions, a reality that can hardly be ignored by governments.

Such impacts on the part of accounting firms and other international business organizations have been described as an emerging "borderless world" with interlinked economies (Ohmae, 1990). Forces at work with considerable success in the international economy are making strong inroads into the economic independence of nations. Such a world system is having unavoidable impacts upon rich and poor nations alike. In Third World jurisdictions, those concerned with developmental issues are finding their policy options constrained by this new economic reality.

In the accounting sphere, changes within individual jurisdictions are influenced by internal economic adjustments, but outside influences are also significant (Samuels and Pifer, 1985, 30). It has been suggested that international service firms can easily adapt their offerings to local markets in ways that give them a competitive edge over potential domestic competitors (Porter, 1990, 266).

In spite of the pressures emanating from the global economy, accounting and auditing standards remain basically under the control of local jurisdictions. Thus wide variations in reporting practices, for example company financial statements, are still in evidence from country to country. This hardly squares with the new realities of the international economy. Although, as mentioned earlier in this chapter, the international accounting firms do exercise considerable control over various professional practices, the regulatory environment may vary between jurisdictions. Some permit private professional organizations to establish standards. Although such standards are presumably reviewed by a national agency, the international firms would appear to have strong influences under such operating procedures.

There are still jurisdictions where standards are set by law or indirectly through government bodies. Whether such autonomous procedures can sustain themselves in the face of strengthening international linkages remains to be seen. Some nations gear accounting standards to taxation, central planning, or other public objectives. Whether or not such practices can be maintained will depend upon the degree of international linkage deemed desirable by domestic policymakers and upon what those policymakers are willing to do to maintain the linkage at that level. At present, wide variations between jurisdictions still exist with respect to how accounting standards are set.

Despite underpinnings for such differences which seem quite rational in a historical sense (Chapters 2 and 8), they may become constraints upon the operating efficiency of the economies concerned (Arpan and Radebaugh, 1985, 13). As suggested earlier (Chapter 8), it is well and good in theory to make generous allowances for the real or felt needs of local circumstances in judging accounting standards but that will not insure a successful role for the nation concerned in the world economy.

The role of accounting services in the international economy dictates the need for public and private interests in various jurisdictions to be able to deal with an accounting profession, the services from which have some degree of consistency. In particular Third World locations, the accounting firms have positioned themselves in keeping with their competitive needs as they seek to satisfy their customers who may also be multinational firms. Their emergence in specific Third World nations cannot be presumed to occur in response to the domestic needs of host economies. Policies that might attract them to specific locations in the absence of the needs of their international clientele are less than obvious.

In meeting the needs of their clients, however, the accounting firms may impact the economies in which they choose to locate. This can occur if they begin to service strictly local clients as a by-product of their main business interests. In doing so, they may bring foreign operating modes to bear upon the host economy. Depending upon the size and sophistication of the economy in question, the international accounting firms may have major impacts upon the shaping of local business services and perhaps even the local economy. Certainly local development planners should be assessing the significance of this on a continuing basis.

Multinational business interests require dependable financial information concerning matters internal to nations where they have current interests and where there are jurisdictions that might come into play in their expansion plans. Third World nations with opportunities to host facilities run by multinational corporations or to otherwise encourage improved international linkages may be in no position to renege on such options. Thus it may well be in the interests of the nations concerned to encourage their accounting subsectors to achieve visible conformity with acceptable international standards. What this may mean in terms of needed adjustments will vary from nation to nation. As emphasized earlier (Chapter 9), the price of development is becoming stronger international linkages and, with them, less domestic control. It has been the international service sector, including its accounting components, that has made the linkage option, however unpalatable, feasible.

Another area of concern for development planners in Third World jurisdictions involves auditing standards. Since these differ internationally, they must be considered. Sound auditing practices provide independent verification when resources are owned by individuals who do not control them or where public concerns are at risk. Auditing and financial reporting vary in the quality of their regulation from country to country with obvious implications for those wishing to do business and for those concerned with economic development. Even where such practices are acceptable domestically, they may lack comparability on the international scene, thus creating difficulties. Since the needs of corporate decision makers transcend national boundaries, nations wishing to host operating units of multinational firms must insure the existence of acceptable auditing services.

Pressures are already in place in the global economy that are seeking to harmonize if not to standardize accounting procedures (Chapters 2 and 8). Of course, complete standardization would further erode the sovereignty of individual nations over their economic affairs. Harmonization, however, would permit a more comfortable adherence to the real or felt needs of specific economies while, at the same time, would facilitate linkages with the international economy. Governments that encourage harmonization presumably will render development more feasible while those that do not will add to the pressures toward standardization. This situation will ultimately give smaller or weaker economies much less say in resolving the problem.

Practices that may appear to be indispensable if the global economy is to function in a reasonable fashion may seem to be far from reasonable in some nations. If the nations concerned reject or cut back the practices in question, they may run the risk of interfering with growth and development. Thus a dilemma has emerged in various Third World nations. Resistance may block expansion, while acceptance may do violence to valued traditions.

In spite of all this, the emergence of the accounting firms in Third World economies seems to suggest better linkages with the international scene for those economies and thus better prospects for development. The improved linkages can impact technology transfer. The firms may generate a demonstration effect in host nations whereby record-keeping procedures and even general business practices are improved. Interactions by the firms with local business interests show them ways in which they can adapt their services to local markets.

Although it appears as though the international accounting firms are playing a positive part in facilitating business operations in the world economy, their success in that regard may not be viewed with immediate favor by governments that are experiencing difficulties from financial innovations that assist corporations in dealing with taxes or restrictions imposed by those governments. When the firms perform such services, there is no doubt that they are breaking down the barriers of economic sovereignty. Wealthier nations, as well as those in the Third World, are experiencing incursions into their sovereignty that are being facilitated by accounting practices initiated by the firms as well as within the domains of multinational corporations.

An important example of this is the practice of transfer pricing. That procedure can be used by corporations for tax avoidance and for cash transfers. Clearly it can be at cross-purposes to the goals and policy objectives of governments. Among its objectives cited earlier in this volume are, in addition to the minimization of taxes and import duties, the avoidance of financial restrictions and the management of currency fluctuations (Mueller, Gernon, and Meek, 1991, 128). It impacts corporate operations in the Third World. Specific nations may attempt to counter it with various restrictions (Chapter 9), but too much success in that regard may limit their opportunities to host corporate facilities. As emphasized earlier, even the threat of transfer pricing creates problems for Third World nations by creating pressure to conform to the standards of the developed world (Lall, 1973, 416).

It was the integration of the world economy that was made feasible through advances in transportation and communications that has facilitated the emergence of the accounting firms as strong international players. In attempting to satisfy the needs of their internationalized clients, they themselves have become a part of the linking mechanisms that hold the global economy together. Their traditional audit functions contribute to the confidence of individual firms operating on the international scene. As they have moved into Third World jurisdictions, there is little doubt that they have facilitated the operations of the clients who brought them there and, in so doing, have initiated or strengthened the linkages that Third World host nations have with the world economy.

In such jurisdictions, those who are reluctant to see growing linkages to the international scene may view the accounting firms and perhaps other services geared to external linkage with some apprehension. Even in wealthy economies, some policymakers are reluctant to cast their lot for linkage beyond their boundaries. In smaller and poorer nations, economic isolation may be an expensive luxury. It seems clear that Third

World nations in general have much to gain by cooperating with the various service groupings that are facilitating the operations of the world economy.

In the case of accounting services, such cooperation would appear to suggest the adoption of policies geared to encourage the harmonization of local accounting standards with international norms. Doing so would presumably make the jurisdictions concerned more attractive to multi-national business interests. This is not a recommendation for Third World nations to court multinational corporations indiscriminantly. Each proposed facility must be assessed on the basis of what positive contribution it can make to the developmental needs of the jurisdiction in question. This is a task that lies well beyond the parameters of the current discussion. The point to be made here is that, by their very existence, the accounting firms and other services geared toward the international economy increase the potential of multinational firms wanting to locate in specific jurisdictions. By doing that, they add to the choices of policymakers seeking to host industry.

As discussed earlier in this book, by moving in the direction of providing various consulting services, the accounting firms are expanding their role as facilitators. By making information available to potential clients concerning what specific jurisdictions have to offer, they are increasing the potential that corporate interests will locate in such settings. Of course the consulting menus that the firms are offering today go well beyond the provision of such information. It would appear that Third World policymakers should keep abreast of what the firms are offering with an eye to encouraging what seems advantageous to them.

If governmental agencies become major clients for the consulting offerings of the firms, then such alliances may have direct developmental impacts. Clearly the agencies concerned must assess the utility of such arrangements on a case-by-case basis. It would seem that both the firms and the governmental agencies in question will be best served if reasonable developmental practices are encouraged. Indeed, reason-ableness in pursuing international linkages would seem to be at the basis of what Third World policymakers should be about in facilitating the emergence of the accounting firms and other international service cadres in their jurisdictions. Both prudence and courage would appear to be indicated.

Selected Bibliography

Abdallah, Wagdy M. (1984) *International Accountability: An International Emphasis*, Ann Arbor, Michigan: UMI Research Press.

Accountancy (1990) "EC Obstacle to Harmonisation," *Accountancy*, Vol. 107, May, p. 12.

Accountants International Study Group (1975) *Professional Accounting in 30 Countries*, New York: AICPA.

Accounting Standards Committee (1980) *Statement of Standard Accounting Practice No. 16: Current Cost Accounting*, London: Accounting Standards Committee.

Agami, Abdel M., and Felix P. Kollaritsch (1983) *Annotated International Accounting Bibliography 1972–1981*, Sarasota, Florida: American Accounting Association.

AlHashim, Dhia D., and Jeffrey S. Arpan (1988) *International Dimensions of Accounting*, 2nd ed., Boston: PWS-Kent Publishing Company.

Aliber, Robert Z. (1973) *The International Money Game*, 5th ed., New York: Basic Books.

American Accounting Association (1973) "Committee on International Accounting, Report," Reprinted in G. M. Scott (Ed.) *An Introduction to Financial Control and Reporting in Multinational Enterprises*, Austin, Texas: University of Texas.

_____ (1976a) "Report of the Committee on Accounting in Developing Countries," *The Accounting Review*, Vol. 51 (Supplement).

_____ (1976b) "Committee on International Accounting. Report 1974–75," *The Accounting Review*, Vol. 51 (Supplement).

_____ (1976c) "Report of the American Accounting Association Committee on International Accounting Operations and Education, 1975–1976," *The Accounting Review*, Vol. 52 (Supplement).

_____ (1978) *Accounting Education and the Third World*, Report of the Committee on International Accounting Operations and Education, 1976–1978, Sarasota, Florida: American Accounting Association.

Arpan, Jeffrey S. (1972) *International Intracorporate Pricing: Non-American Systems and Views*, New York: Praeger.

Arpan, Jeffrey S., and Lee H. Radebaugh (1985) *International Accounting and Multinational Enterprises*, 2nd ed., New York: John Wiley & Sons.

Arthur Andersen & Company (1963) *The First Fifty Years 1913–1963*, Chicago: Arthur Andersen & Company. Reprint 1984, New York: Garland Publishing.

Baer, W., and L. Samuelson (1981) "Toward a Service Oriented Growth Strategy," *World Development*, Vol. 9, No. 6, pp. 499–514.

Barcet, A., and J. Bonamy (1983) "Differenciation des prestations de services aux enterprises," *Revue d'Economie Industrielle*, No. 24, 2nd Trimester, pp. 9–17.

Bavishi, Vinod B. (1981) "Capital Budgeting Practices at Multinationals," *Management Accountant*, Vol. 63, August, pp. 32–35.

_____ (1983) *Who Audits the World: Trends in the Worldwide Auditing Profession*, Princeton, New Jersey: Center for International Financial Analysis and Research, Inc.

_____ (1989) *International Accounting and Auditing Trends*, Vol. 1 & Vol. 2, Princeton, New Jersey: Center for International Financial Analysis and Research, Inc.

Bearse, P. J. (1978) "On the Intra-Regional Diffusion of Business Services Activity," *Regional Studies*, Vol. 12, No. 5, pp. 563–78.

Belkaoui, Ahmed (1985) *International Accounting: Issues and Solutions*, Westport, Connecticut: Quorum Books.

_____ (1988) *The New Environment of International Accounting: Issues and Practices*, New York: Quorum Books.

Bell, Daniel (1973) *The Coming of Post-Industrial Society*, New York: Basic Books.

Benz, S. F. (1989) "Trade Liberalization and the Global Service Economy," *Journal of World Trade Law*, Vol. 19, March/April, pp. 95–120.

Berton, Lee (1986a) "Peat Marwick KMG Main Agree to Merge," *Wall Street Journal*, September 4, p. 3.

_____ (1986b) "Peat-KMG Merger Will Form a Goliath," *Wall Street Journal*, September 12, p. 6.

_____ (1989a) "Talk of Mergers Sweeps Through Accounting Field," *Wall Street Journal*, June 19, p. A5A.

_____ (1989b) "Arthur Andersen, Price Waterhouse Say They're in Formal Discussions on Merger," *Wall Street Journal*, July 7, p. A6.

Berton, Lee, and Jonathan B. Schiff (1990) *Wall Street Journal on Accounting*, Homewood, Illinois: Dow Jones-Irwin.

Bhagwati, J. N. (1984) "Splintering and Disembodiment of Services and Developing Nations," *World Economy*, Vol. 7, No. 2, pp. 133–43.

Bhalla, A. S. (1970) "The Role of Services in Employment Expansion," *International Labor Review*, Vol. 101, No. 5, pp. 529–39.

_____ (1973) "A Disaggregative Approach to LDC's Tertiary Sector," *Journal of Development Studies*, Vol. 10.

Biggs, Sheridan C., Jr. (1986) "The Changing Economics of the Public Accounting Profession," *The Ohio CPA*, Vol. 45, Summer, pp. 11–18.

Birnbaum, Jeffrey H. (1989) "Accounting Concerns Assume Burgeoning Role as Lobbyists, Often Outshoot Federal Bureaucrats," *Wall Street Journal*, March 7, p. A26.

Blair, P. M. (1980) "Implications of Growth in Services for Social Structure," *Social Science Quarterly*, Vol. 61, No. 1, pp. 3–22.

Bloom, Robert, and M. S. Naciri (1989) "Accounting Standard Setting and Culture: A Comparative Analysis of the United States, Canada, England, West Germany,

Australia, New Zealand, Sweden, Japan, and Switzerland," *International Journal of Accounting*, Vol. 24, Spring, pp. 70–97.

Boys, Peter (1989) "What's in a Name" *Accountancy*, Vol. 103, January, pp. 100–3.

_____ (1990) "What's in a Name: Update," *Accountancy*, Vol. 105, March, pp. 132–34.

Brennan, W. John (1979) *The Internationalization of the Accountancy Profession*, Toronto, Canada: Institute of Chartered Accountants.

Brief, Richard P. (1986) *Accounting Thought and Practice Through the Years*, New York: Garland Publishing.

Briston, Richard J. (1978) "The Evolution of Accounting in Developing Countries," *International Journal of Accounting Education and Research*, Vol. 14, Fall.

Bromwich, M., and A. G. Hopwood (Eds.) (1983) *Accounting Standards Setting: An International Perspective*, London: Pitman.

Brown, Richard (1905) *A History of Accounting and Accountants*, Edinburgh and London: T. C. and E. C. Jack. Reprint 1971, New York: Augustus M. Kelley.

Burns, Jane O. (1980) "Transfer Pricing Decisions in US Multinational Corporations," *Journal of International Business Studies*, Fall, pp. 23–39.

Burns, Joseph M. (1976) *Accounting Standards and International Finance*, Washington D. C.: American Enterprise Institute of Public Policy Research.

Burton, John C. (Ed.) (1981) *The International World of Accounting: Challenges and Opportunities*, New York: Arthur Young.

Business International (1974) *Solving Accounting Problems for Worldwide Operations*, New York: Business International.

_____ (1984) *Coping with the Worldwide Accounting Changes: Successful Strategies and Techniques for the 1980s*, New York: Business International.

Bywater, M. F., and B. S. Yamey (1982) *Historic Accounting Literature: A Companion Guide*, London: Scholar Press.

Cairns, David (1988) "Calling all National Standard Setters," *Accountancy*, Vol. 104, February, pp. 13–14.

_____ (1989) "IASC's Blueprint for the Future" *Accountancy*, Vol. 104, December, pp. 80–82.

_____ (1990) "Aid for the Developing World," *Accountancy*, Vol. 105, March, pp. 82–85.

Campbell, Leslie G. (1985) *International Auditing*, New York: St. Martin's Press.

Carey, Anthony (1990) "Harmonisation: Europe Moves Forward," *Accountancy*, Vol. 105, March, pp. 92–93.

Carey, John L. (1969) *The Rise of the Accounting Profession*, New York: American Institute of Certified Public Accountants.

_____ (1970) "How can Barriers Against International Accounting Practice be Eliminated?" *International Journal of Accounting*, Vol. 6, Fall, pp. 53–58.

Castle, Leslie, and Christopher Findley (Eds.) (1988) *Pacific Trade in Services*, Sydney: Allen & Unwin.

Chandler, Roy (1989) "Setting Standards for the World," *The Accountant's Magazine*, Vol. 93, July, pp. 43–44.

_____ (1990) "IFAC: The Consensus-Seekers," *Accountancy*, Vol. 106, July, pp. 84–86.

Chatfield, Michael (Ed.) (1968) *Contemporary Studies in the Evolution of Accounting Thought*, Belmont, California: Dickenson Publishing Company.

Chetkovich, M. N. (1979) "The International Federation of Accountants: Its Organisation and Goals," *International Journal of Accounting*, Vol. 15, Fall, pp. 13–20.

Choi, Frederick D. S. (1974) "European Disclosure: The Competitive Disclosure Hypotheses," *Journal of International Business Studies*, Vol. 5, Fall, pp. 15–23.

_____ (1979) "ASEAN Federation of Accountants: A New International Accounting Force," *International Journal of Accounting*, Vol. 15, Fall, pp. 53–75.

_____ (1980) "Primary-Secondary Reporting: A Cross-Cultural Analysis," *International Journal of Accounting, Education, and Research*, Vol. 16, Fall, pp. 83–104.

_____ (1981) *Multinational Accounting. A Research Framework for the Eighties*, Ann Arbor, Michigan: UMI Research Press.

_____ (1981) "A Cluster Approach to Accounting Harmonization," *Management Accounting*, Vol. 63, August, pp. 26–31.

Choi, Frederick D. S., and Vinod B. Bavishi (1982a) "Diversity in Multinational Accounting," *Financial Executive*, Vol. 50, August, pp. 45–49.

_____ (1982b) "Financial Accounting Standards: A Multinational Synthesis and Policy Framework," *International Journal of Accounting*, Vol. 18, Fall, pp. 159–83.

_____ (1983) "International Accounting Standards: Issues Needing Attention," *Journal of Accountancy*, Vol. 155, March, pp. 62–68.

Choi, Frederick D. S., and Richard M. Levich (1990) *The Capital Market Effects of International Accounting Diversity*, New York: Dow-Jones & Company, Inc.

Choi, Frederick D. S., and G. G. Mueller (1984) *International Accounting*, Englewood Cliffs, New Jersey: Prentice-Hall.

_____ (Eds.) (1979) *Essentials of Multinational Accounting, An Anthology*, Ann Arbor, Michigan: University Microfilms International.

Clairmonte, F., and J. Cavanagh (1984) "Transnational Corporations and Services: The Final Frontier," *Trade and Development*, Vol. 5, pp. 215–73.

Clark, Gordon L., Meric S. Gertler, and John Whiteman (1986) *Regional Dynamics: Studies in Adjustment Theory*, Boston: Allen and Unwin.

Cohen, Stephen S., and John Zysman (1987) *Manufacturing Matters: The Myth of Post-Industrial Society*, New York: Basic Books.

Congress of the United States (1986) *Trade in Services, Exports and Foreign Revenues: Special Report*, Washington D.C..: Government Printing Office.

Cook, Allan (1989) "International Business: A Channel for Change in United Kingdom Accounting," in Anthony G. Hopwood (Ed.). *International Pressures for Accounting Change*, Hemel Hempstead: Prentice-Hall International (UK) Ltd.

Cooper, Ernest (1921) *Fifty-seven Years in an Accountant's Office*, Oxford, England: Gee & Co. Reprint 1982, New York: Garland Publishing.

Coopers & Lybrand (1984) *The Early History of Coopers & Lybrand*, New York: Coopers & Lybrand.

Costouros, George J. (1979) *Accounting in the Golden Age of Greece: A Response to Socioeconomic Changes*, Urbana, Illinois: Center for International Education and Research in Accounting.

Coulson, Ed (1989) "Seeing Eye to Eye," *CA Magazine*, Vol. 122, September, p. 36.

DaCosta, R. C., J. C. Bourgeois, and W. M. Lawson (1978) "Linkages in the International Business Community: Accounting Evidence," *International Journal of Accounting Education and Research*, Vol. 13, Spring, pp. 73–85.

Daley, L., and G. Mueller (1982) "Accounting in the Arena of World Politics," *Journal of Accountancy*, Vol. 153, February, pp. 40–50.

Daniels, P. W. (1982) *Service Industries*, Cambridge: Cambridge University Press, 1982.

_____ (1985) "The Geography of Services," *Progress in Human Geography*, Vol. 9, No. 3, pp. 443–51.

_____ (1986) "Foreign Banks and Metropolitan Development: A Comparison of London and New York," *Tijdschrift voor economische en sociale geografie*, Vol. 77, No. 4, pp. 269–87.

Daniels, P. W., A. Leyshon, and N. J. Thrift (1988) "Large Accountancy Firms in the UK: Operational Adaptation and Spatial Development," *The Service Industries Journal*, Vol. 8, No. 3, pp. 317–46.

Doyle, P., and M. Corstjens (1983) "Optimal Growth Strategies for Service Organizations," *Journal of Business*, Vol. 56, No. 3, pp. 389–405.

Dufey, G., and I. Giddy (1978a) *The International Money Market*, Englewood Cliffs, New Jersey: Prentice-Hall.

_____ (1978b) "International Financial Planning: The Use of Market-Based Forecasts," *California Management Review*, Vol. 21, Fall, pp. 69–81.

Eckstein, H. J., and D. M. Heier (1985) "Causes and Consequences of Service Sector Growth: The U.S. Experience," *Growth and Change*, Vol. 16, No. 2, pp. 12–17.

The Economist (1983) "Price Waterhouse: A New Way to Pay Old Debts," *The Economist*, Vol. 287, May 7, p. 93.

_____ (1985) "Felled Auditors: Melbourne," *The Economist*, Vol. 294, March 30, p. 84.

_____ (1989a) "Who Will Audit the Auditors?" *The Economist*, Vol. 312, July 15, p. 18.

_____ (1989b) "Accountancy Mergers 1 + 1 = 1," *The Economist*, Vol. 311, May 27, pp. 82–84.

Edey, H. C. (1982) *Accounting Queries*, New York: Garland Publishing Inc.

Edwards, James Don (1960) *History of Public Accounting in the United States*, East Lansing: Michigan State University.

Edwards, James Don, and Barbara J. Shildneck (1987) "The AICPA's First Century," *Management Accounting*, Vol. 69, September, pp. 57–61.

Effros, Robert C. (Ed.) (1982) *Emerging Financial Centers: Legal and Institutional Framework*, Washington, D. C.: International Monetary Fund.

Emerson, James C. (1988) *Careers in Public Accounting*, Redmond, Washington: The Big Eight Review, Inc.

Enthoven, Adolf J. H. (1980a) "The Accountant in the Third World," *Journal of Accountancy*, Vol. 149, March, pp. 76–78.

_____ (1980b) "International Management Accounting — A Challenge for Accountants," *Management Accounting*, Vol. 62, September, pp. 25–32.

_____ (1982) "International Management Accounting: Its Scope and Standards," *The International Journal of Accounting, Education, and Research*, Vol. 17, Spring, pp. 59–74.

Ernst & Whinney (1979) *Worldwide Statutory Audit and Reporting Requirements*, Cleveland, Ohio: Ernst & Whinney.

_____ (1981) *Foreign Exchange Rates and Restrictions: International Series*, Cleveland, Ohio: Ernst and Whinney.

_____ (1982) *International Accounting Standards*, Cleveland, Ohio: Ernst and Whinney.

Euromoney (1986) "To List or Not to List?" *Euromoney Supplement (Selling Equities to the World)*, November, pp. 43–45.

Evans, Thomas G., Martin E. Taylor, and Oscar Holzmann (1985) *International Accounting and Reporting*, New York: MacMillan.

Falk, L. H., and A. Broner (1980) "Specialization in Service Industry Employment as a State Policy," *Growth and Change*, Vol. 11, No. 4, pp. 18–23.

Fantl, Irving L. (1971) "The Case Against International Uniformity," *Management Accounting*, Vol. 52, May, pp. 13–16.

Farmer, R., and B. Richman (1966) *International Business: An Operational Theory*, Homewood, Illinois: Irwin.

Feketekuty, Geza (1988) *International Trade in Services*, Cambridge, Massachusetts: Ballinger.

Financial Accounting Standards Board (1975) "Accounting for the Translation of Foreign Currency Transactions and Foreign Currency Financial Statements," *Statement of Financial Accounting Standards No. 8*, Stamford, Connecticut: Financial Accounting Standards Board.

_____ (1976) "Financial Reporting for Segments of a Business Enterprise," *Statement of Financial Accounting Standards No. 14*, Stamford, Connecticut: Financial Accounting Standards Board.

_____ (1979) "Financial Reporting and Changing Prices," *Statement of Financial Accounting Standards No. 33*, Stamford, Connecticut: Financial Accounting Standards Board.

_____ (1981) "Foreign Currency Translation," *Statement of Financial Accounting Standards No. 52*, Stamford, Connecticut: Financial Accounting Standards Board.

Fitzgerald, R. D. (1981) "International Harmonization of Accounting and Reporting," *International Journal of Accounting*, Vol. 17, Fall, pp. 21–32.

Forsyth, David J. C. (1990) *Technology Policy for Small Developing Countries*, New York: St. Martin's Press.

Fox, Samuel, and Norlin G. Rueschhoff (1986) *Principles of International Accounting*, Austin, Texas: Austin Press.

Frank, W. G. (1979) "An Empirical Analysis of International Accounting Principles," *Journal of Accounting Research*, Vol. 17, Autumn, pp. 593–605.

Gavin, B. (1985) "A GATT for International Banking?" *Journal of World Trade Law*, Vol. 19, March/April, pp. 121–35.

Gemmell, Norman (1982) "Economic Development and Structural Change: The Role of the Service Sector," *The Journal of Development Studies*, Vol. 19, No. 1, pp. 37–67.

Geow, G. F. H. (1979) "The Service Sector in Singapore's Economy: Performance and Structure," *Malayan Economic Review*, Vol. 24, No. 2, pp. 46–73.

Germidis, Dimitri, and Charles Albert Michalet (1984) *International Banks and Financial Markets in Developing Countries*, Paris: OECD Development Center Studies.

Gershuny, Jonathan (1978) *After Industrial Society? The Emerging Self Service Economy*, Atlantic Highlands, New Jersey: Humanities Press, 1978.

Gershuny, Jonathan, and I. D. Miles (1983) *The New Service Economy: The Transformation of Employment in Industrial Societies*, New York: Praeger.

Goodrich, P. S. (1982) "A Typology of International Accounting Principles and Policies," *AUTA Review*, cited in Nobes (1983).

Gray, S. J. (1980) "The Impact of International Accounting Differences from a Security-Analysis Perspective: Some European Evidence," *Journal of Accounting Research*, Vol. 18, Spring, pp. 64–76.

———— (Ed.) (1983) *International Accounting and Transnational Decisions*, London: Butterworth.

Gray, S. J., L. G. Campbell, and J. C. Shaw (1984) *International Financial Reporting, a Comparative International Survey of Accounting Requirements and Practices in 30 Countries*, New York: St. Martin's Press.

Gray, S. J., and A. G. Coenenberg (Eds.) (1984) *EEC Accounting Harmonisation: Implementation and Impact of the Fourth Directive*, Amsterdam: North-Holland.

Gray, S. J., L. B. McSweeney, and J. C. Shaw (1984) *Information Disclosure and the Multinational Corporation*, New York: John Wiley and Sons.

Gray, S. J., Jack C. Shaw, and Brendan McSweeney (1981) "Accounting Standards and Multinational Corporations," *Journal of International Business Studies*, Vol. 12, Spring/Summer, pp. 121–36.

Gupta, Udayan (1989) "Big Eight Competing for Little Guy in Effort to Grow," *Wall Street Journal*, January 17, p. B2.

Hampton, Robert (1980) "A World of Differences in Accounting and Reporting," *Management Accounting*, Vol. 62, September, pp. 14–18.

Hatfield, H. R. (1966) "Some Variations in Accounting Practices in England, France, Germany, and the U.S.," *Journal of Accounting Research*, Vol. 4, Autumn, pp. 169–82.

Helleiner, G. K. (1973) "Manufacturing Exports from Less Developed Countries and Multinational Firms," *The Economic Journal*, Vol. 83, No. 329, pp. 21–47.

Hemp, Paul (1985) "Where Boards and Governments Have Failed, the Market Could Internationalize Accounting," *Wall Street Journal*, May 8, p. 34.

Hermann, B., and B. van Holst (1984) *International Trade in Services: Some Theoretical and Practical Problems*, Rotterdam: Netherlands Economic Institute.

Holtzblatt, Mark A., and Samuel Fox (1983) "The Basic International Accounting Dilemma: Uniformity vs. Harmonization," *Business and Society*, Vol. 22, Spring, pp. 43–48.

Holzer, H. P. (Ed.) (1984) *International Accounting*, New York: Harper & Row.

Holzer, H. P., and H. M. Schoenfeld (Eds.) (1986) *Managerial Accounting and Analysis in Multinational Enterprises*, Berlin: Walter de Gruyter.

Hopwood, Anthony G. (Ed.) (1989) *International Pressures for Accounting Change*, Hemel Hempstead: Prentice Hall International (UK) Ltd.

Horner, Larry D. (1986) "The New Rosetta Stone," *The Ohio CPA*, Vol. 45, Autumn, pp. 5–7.

Hove, M. (1982) "Why Accountancy is Failing the Third World," *Certified Accountant*, Vol. 74, October, pp. 44–45.

Institutional Investor (1989) "The International Stock Exchange Directory," *Institutional Investor*, Vol. 23, March, pp. 197–204.

Internal Auditor (1991) "Internal Audit Neglected in Britain?" *The Internal Auditor*, Vol. 48, October, p. 11.

International Accounting Standards Committee (1981) "Information Reflecting the Effects of Changing Prices," *International Accounting Standards*. Reprinted in American Institute of Certified Public Accountants (1991) *International Accounting and Auditing Standards*, Chicago: Commerce Clearing House, Inc.

International Trade Administration, U.S. Department of Commerce (1988) *International Direct Investment: Global Trends and the U.S. Role*, Washington, D.C.: U.S. Government Printing Office.

_____ (1989) *United States Trade: Performance in 1988*, Washington, D.C.: U.S. Government Printing Office.

Jameson, Kenneth P. (1977) "The Development of the Service Industry: An Empirical Investigation," *Quarterly Review of Economics and Business*, Vol. 17, No. 10, pp. 31–40.

Jéquier, Nocolas, and Yao-Su Hu (1989) *Banking and the Promotion of Technological Development*, New York: St. Martin's Press.

Journal of Accountancy (1990) "Support for International Standards," *Journal of Accountancy*, Vol. 169, April, pp. 15–16.

_____ (1991) "New International Accounting Standards Volume Offered," *Journal of Accountancy*, Vol. 171, June, p. 20.

Jussawalla, Meheroo, Tadayuki Okama, and Toshihiro Araki (Eds.) (1989) *Information Technology and Global Interdependence*, Westport, Connecticut: Greenwood Press.

Kagle, Arthur R., Takamiki Fujimoto, and Seiichiro Shimogaki (1988) "Audit Needs of the Japanese Corporation," *The Internal Auditor*, Vol. 45, April, pp. 51–53.

Kanaga, William (1980) "International Accounting: The Challenge and the Changes," *Journal of Accountancy*, Vol. 150, November, pp. 55–61.

Katouzian, M. A. (1970) "The Development of the Service Sector: A New Approach," *Oxford Economic Papers*, New Series, Vol. 22, No. 3, November, pp. 362–82.

Keefe, Gary L. (1989) "Helping Clients Prepare for Global Markets," *Journal of Accountancy*, Vol. 168, July, pp. 54–65.

Keister, O. R. (1965) "The Mechanics of Mesopotamian Record Keeping," *National Association of Accountants Bulletin*, February, pp. 18–24. Reprinted in M. Chatfield (Ed.) (1968) *Contemporary Studies on the Evolution of Accounting Thought*, Belmont, California: Dickenson Publishing Co.

Kettle, Russell, Sir (1958) *Deloitte & Co. 1845–1956*, Oxford, England: Deloitte, Plender, Griffiths. Reprint 1984, New York: Garland Publishers.

Kolde, Endel-Jakob (1982) *Environment of International Business*, Kent, Ohio: Kent State University Press.

Kuhlberg, Duane R. (1981) "Management of a Multinational Public Accounting Firm," *International Journal of Accounting Education and Research*, Vol. 17, Fall, pp. 1–6.

Lall, Sanjaya (1973) "Transfer Pricing by Multinational Manufacturing Firms," *Oxford Bulletin of Economics and Statistics*. Reprinted in S. J. Gray (Ed.) (1983) *International Accounting and Transnational Decisions*, London: Butterworth.

_____ (1984) "Transnationals and the Third World: Changing Perceptions," *National Westminster Bank Quarterly Review*, May, pp. 2–16.

Langdon, William E. (1986) "An International Viewpoint," *CMA Magazine*, Vol. 50, March–April, p. 58.

Leyshon, A., P. W. Daniels, and N. S. Thrift (1987a) "Large Accountancy Firms in the UK: Operational Adaptation and Spatial Development," *Working Papers on Producer Services, No. 2*, St. David's University College: Lampeter and University of Liverpool.

_____ (1987b) "Internationalization of Professional Producer Services: The Case of Large Accountancy Firms," *Working Papers on Producer Services, No. 3*, March, St. David's University: Lampeter and University of Liverpool.

Littleton, A. C. (1933) *Accounting Evolution to 1900*, New York: American Institute Publishing Company. Reissued 1966. New York: Russell and Russell.

Littleton, A. C., and B. S. Yamey (1956) *Studies in the History of Accounting*, Homewood, Illinois: Richard D. Irwin, Inc.

Louis, Arthur M. (1968) "The Accountants Are Changing the Rules," *Fortune*, Vol. 77, June 15, pp. 177–79, 330, 336, 339, and 346.

May, George O. (1936) *Twenty-five Years of Accounting Responsibility*, New York: American Institute Publishing Company, Inc.

McKee, David L. (1977) "Facteurs extérieurs et infrastructure des pays en voie de développment," *Revue Tiers-Monde*, Vol. 18, No. 70, pp. 293–300.

_____ (1988) *Growth, Development and the Service Economy in the Third World*, New York: Praeger.

_____ (1991) *Schumpeter and the Political Economy of Change*, New York: Praeger.

McKee, David L., and Richard E. Bennett (Eds.) (1987) *Structural Change in an Urban Industrial Region*, New York: Praeger.

McKee, David L., and Clem Tisdell (1990) *Developmental Issues in Small Island Economies*, New York: Praeger.

Meek, Gary (1989) *An Overview of International Financial Accounting*. Unpublished paper delivered at American Assembly of Collegiate Schools of Business Meeting.

Miller, Elwood (1979) *Accounting Problems of Multinational Enterprises*, Lexington, Massachusetts: D.C. Heath and Company.

_____ (1982) *Responsibility Accounting and Performance Evaluations*, New York: Van Nostrand Reinhold Company.

Montgomery, Robert H. (1939) *Fifty Years of Accountancy*, New York: Ronald Press.

Moyer, C. A. (1951) "Early Developments in American Auditing," *The Accounting Review*, Vol. 26, January, pp. 3–8.

Mueller, Gerhard G. (1967) *International Accounting*, New York: Macmillan.

_____ (1968) "Accounting Principles Generally Accepted in the U.S. Versus Those Generally Accepted Elsewhere," *International Journal of Accounting*, Vol. 3, Spring, pp. 91–103.

Mueller, Gerhard G., Helen Gernon, and Gary Meek (1991) *Accounting: An International Perspective*, Homewood, Illinois: Irwin.

Mueller, Gerhard G., and Lauren M. Walker (1976) "The Coming of Age of Transnational Financial Reporting," *Journal of Accountancy*, Vol. 142, July.

Nair, R. D., and Werner G. Frank (1980) "The Impact of the Disclosure and Measurement Practices on International Accounting Classifications," *The Accounting Review*, Vol. 55, July, pp. 426–50.

―――― (1981) "The Harmonization of International Accounting Standards 1973–1979," *International Journal of Accounting*, Vol. 17, Fall, pp. 61–77.

―――― (1982) "Empirical Guidelines for Comparing International Accounting Data," *Journal of International Business Studies*, Vol. 13, Winter, pp. 85–98.

National Association of Accountants (1974) *Management Accounting for Multinational Corporations*, Volumes I and II, New York: National Association of Accountants.

Nobes, C. W. (1981) "An Empirical Analysis of International Accounting Principles: A Comment," *Journal of Accounting Research*, Spring.

―――― (1983) "A Judgmental International Classification of Financial Reporting Practices," *Journal of Business Finance and Accounting*, Vol. 10, Spring, pp. 1–19.

―――― (1986a) "Is the IASC Worthwhile?" *International Accounting Bulletin*, February.

―――― (1986b) *Issues in International Accounting*, New York: Garland Publishing.

―――― (1987) "Classification of Financial Reporting Practices," *Advances in International Accounting*, Vol. 1, pp. 1–22.

―――― (1990) "EC Group Accounting: Two Zillion Ways To Do It," *Accountancy*, Vol. 106, December, pp. 84–85.

Nobes, C. W., and J. Matatko (1980) "Classification of National Systems of Financial Accounting," *AUTA Review*, Autumn.

Nobes, C. W., and R. H. Parker (Eds.) (1981) *Comparative International Accounting*, Oxford, England: Irwin.

―――― (1988) *Issues in Multinational Accounting*, New York: St. Martin's Press.

Noyelle, Thierry J., and Anna B. Dutka (1988) *International Trade in Business Services: Accounting, Advertising, Law and Management Consulting*, Cambridge, Massachusetts: Ballinger.

Nusbaumer, Jacques (1987) *Services in the Global Market*, Boston, Massachusetts: Kluwer Academic Publishers.

Ohmae, Kenichi (1990) *The Borderless World: Power and Strategy in the Interlinked Economy*, New York: McKinsey & Company, Inc.

Organization for Economic Cooperation and Development (1980a) "Accounting Standards for International Business," *OECD Observer*, Vol. 104, May, pp. 28–29.

―――― (1980b) *Accounting Practices in OECD Countries*, Paris: OECD.

―――― (1984) *International Trade in Services: Banking*, Paris: OECD.

―――― (1985) *Twenty-Five Years of Development Co-Operation: A Review*, Paris: OECD.

―――― (1986a) *Financial Resources for Developing Countries: 1985 and Recent Trends*, Paris: OECD.

―――― (1986b) *Financial Market Trends*, Paris: OECD.

―――― (1986c) *Geographical Distribution of Financial Flows to Developing Countries: 1981–1989*, Paris: OECD.

Olson, Wallace E. (1980) *The Accounting Profession — Years of Trial: 1969 through 1980*, New York: American Institute of Certified Public Accountants.

Palmer, Russell E. (1989) "Accounting as a Mature Industry," *Journal of Accountancy*, Vol. 167, May, pp. 84–88.

Parker, R. H. (1984) *Papers on Accounting History*, New York: Garland Publishing.

Parry, Thomas G. (1973) "The International Firm and National Economic Policy," *Economic Journal*, Vol. 84, No. 332, pp. 1201–27.

Peat, Marwick, Mitchell & Co. (1986) *Worldwide Financial Reporting and Audit Requirements: A Peat Marwick Inventory*, New York: Peat, Marwick, Mitchell & Co.

Penney, Louis H. (1961) "The Significance of Mergers of Accounting Firms," *The Journal of Accounting*, Vol. 112, November, pp. 51–58.

Peragallo, Edward (1938) *Origin and Evolution of Double Entry Bookkeeping*, New York: American Institute Publishing Company.

Perera, M. H. B. (1989) "Towards a Framework to Analyze the Impact of Culture on Accounting," *The Informational Journal of Accounting Education and Research*, Vol. 24, No. 1, pp. 42–56.

Persen, William, and Van Lessig (1979) *Evaluating the Financial Performance of Overseas Operations*, New York: Financial Executives' Foundation.

Pollard, Sidney (1963) "Capital Accounting in the Industrial Revolution," *Yorkshire Bulletin of Economic and Social Research*, Vol. 15, November, pp. 71–91, reprinted in Michael Chatfield (1969) *Contemporary Studies in the Evolution of Accounting Thought*, Belmont, California: Dickenson Publishing Co.

Porter, Michael E. (1990) *The Competitive Advantage of Nations*, New York: The Free Press.

Previts, Gary John, and Barbara Dubis Merino (1979) *A History of Accounting in America*, New York: John Wiley & Sons.

Price Waterhouse (1973) *Accounting Principles and Reporting Practices: A Survey in 38 Countries*, New York: Price Waterhouse.

_____ (1975) *A Survey in 46 Countries: Accounting Principles and Reporting Practices*, New York: Price Waterhouse International.

_____ (1979) *International Survey of Accounting Principles and Reporting Practices*, New York: Butterworths.

_____ (1980) *International Survey of Accounting Principles and Reporting Practices*, London: Butterworth.

_____ (1988a) *Corporate Taxes, Individual Taxes, Foreign Exchange Investment Regulations: An Asian Pacific Region Summary*, New York: Price Waterhouse.

_____ (1988b) *Doing Business in Fiji*, New York: Price Waterhouse.

_____ (1989) *Doing Business in Barbados*, New York: Price Waterhouse.

Prodhan, Bimal (1986) *Multinational Accounting: Segment Disclosure and Risk*, London: Croom Helm.

Radburn, William F. (1986) "Legislated Internal Audit: Canada's New Provisions," *The Internal Auditor*, Vol. 43, June, pp. 18–24.

Riddle, D. I. (1986) *Service-led Growth: The Role of the Service Sector in World Development*, New York: Praeger.

Robinson, Richard D. (1988) *The International Transfer of Technology: Theory Issues and Practice*, Cambridge, Massachusetts: Ballinger.

Sahlgren, Kaus A. (1979) "The Work of Non-Accountant International Bodies: The United Nations," in W. John Brennan (Ed.) *The Internationalization of the Accountancy Profession*, Toronto: The Canadian Institute of Chartered Accountants.

Sampson, A. (1983) *The Money Launderers: The People and Politics of the World Banking Crisis*, Hammondsworth: Penguin Books.

Samuels, J. M., and J. Oliga (1982) "Accounting Standards in Developing Countries," *International Journal of Accounting*, Vol. 18, Fall, pp. 67–88.

Samuels, J. M., and A. G. Piper (1985) *International Accounting: A Survey*, New York: St. Martin's Press.

Sardinas, Joseph L. Jr., and Susan Merrill (1987) "Regulation of International Data Communications and the Effect Upon Multinational Corporations," *Advances in International Accounting*, Vol. 1, pp. 305–15.

Sasseen, Jane (1984) "Numbers Game: Take the Cash and Let the Standards Go," *Forbes*, Vol. 134, July 2, pp. 180–82.

Scott, George M. (1973) *An Introduction to Financial Control and Reporting in Multinational Enterprises*, Austin: The University of Texas.

_____ (1978) "Planning and Control in International Operations," in Sam R. Goodman and James S. Reece (Eds.) (1978) *Controller's Handbook*, Homewood, Illinois: Dow Jones-Irwin.

Sesit, Michael R., Ann Monroe, and Peter Truell (1986) "Prosperity and Peril in the Brave New Market," *Wall Street Journal*, September 29, pp. 29D–46D.

Shapiro, Alan C. (1978) "Evaluation and Control of Foreign Operations," *The International Journal of Accounting Education and Research*, Vol. 14, Fall, pp. 83–104.

Smith, Randall (1991) "A $100 Million Man Finally Gets Attention, Much to His Chagrin," *Wall Street Journal*, October 11, p. 1

Snow, Marcellus, and Meheroo Jussawalla (1989) "Deregulatory Trends in OECD Countries," in Meheroo Jussawalla, Tadayuki Okama, and Toshihiro Araki (Eds.) *Information Technology and Global Interdependence*, Westport, Connecticut: Greenwood Press, pp. 21–39.

Spero, Joan E. (1989) "The Information Revolution and Financial Services: A New North-South Issue?" in Meheroo Jussawalla, Tadayuki Okama, and Toshihiro Araki (Eds.) *Information Technology and Global Interdependence*, Westport, Connecticut: Greenwood Press.

Stanback, Thomas M., Jr., Peter J. Bearse, Thierry J. Noyelle, and Robert A. Karasek (1981) *Services: The New Economy*, Totowa, New Jersey: Allanheld, Osmun & Co. Publishers, Inc.

Stern, Robert M., and Bernard M. Hoekman (1988) "Issues in International Trade in Services," in Leslie Castle and Christopher Findlay (Eds.) (1988) *Pacific Trade in Services*, Sydney: Allen & Unwin.

Time (1989) "Accounting: The Big Eight, Seven, Six . . . ," *Time*, Vol. 134, July 17, p. 77.

Tucker, Ken, and Mark Sundberg (1988) *International Trade in Services*, New York: Routledge.

United Nations Center on Transnational Corporations (1982) *Towards International Standardization of Corporate Accounting and Reporting*, New York: United

Nations Center on Transnational Corporations.

_____ (1983) *Transnational Corporations in World Development: Third Survey*, New York: United Nations Center on Transnational Corporations.

_____ (1987) *Foreign Direct Investment, the Service Sector and International Banking*, New York: United Nations Center on Transnational Corporations.

U.S. Bureau of the Census (1960) *Statistical Abstract of the United States: 1960*, Washington, D.C.: U.S. Government Printing Office.

_____ (1990) *Statistical Abstract of the United States: 1990*, 110th Ed., Washington, D.C.: U.S. Government Printing Office.

U. S. News & World Report (1989) "Business: Less is More Among the Bean Counters," *U. S. News & World Report*, Vol. 107, No. 3, p. 11.

Van Hulle, Karel (1989) "The EC Experience of Harmonisation: Part 2," *Accountancy*, Vol. 4, October, pp. 96–99.

Vangermeersch, Richard (1985) "The Route of the Seventh Directive of the EEC on Consolidated Accounts — Slow, Steady, Studied, and Successful," *The International Journal of Accounting*, Vol. 20, Spring, 103–18.

Wall Street Journal (1989) "Deloitte Haskins, Touche Approve Merger in U. S.," *Wall Street Journal*, August 14, p. A4.

Watt, George C., Richard M. Hammer, and Marianne Burge (1977) *Accounting for the Multinational Corporation*, Homewood, Illinois: Dow Jones-Irwin.

Weinstein, Arnold K., Louis Corsini, and Ronald Pawliczek (1978) "The Big Eight in Europe," *International Journal of Accounting Education and Research*, Vol. 13, Spring, pp. 57–71.

Wilson, Allister (1991) "US and EC: Harmonisation Through Equivalence," *Accountancy*, Vol. 107, April, pp. 81–82.

Wootton, Charles W. (1990) *The Development of the "Big Eight" Accounting Firms in the United States, 1900 to 1990*, Toronto: American Accounting Association Annual Meeting.

Wu, Frederick, and Donald W. Hackett (1977) "The Internationalization of U.S. Public Accounting Firms," *International Journal of Accounting*, Vol. 12, Spring, pp. 81–91.

Wyatt, Arthur (1989) "International Accounting Standards: A New Perspective," *Accounting Horizons*, Vol. 3, September, pp. 105–8.

Wyman, Harold E. (1989) "The Auditing Profession in Europe," *Accountancy*, Vol. 103, February, pp. 82–87.

Yamey, Basil S. (1982) *Further Essays on the History of Accounting*, New York: Garland Publishing.

Zimmerman, V. K. (1977) *The Multinational Corporation: Accounting and Social Implications*, Urbana, Illinois: University of Illinois.

Index

About the Authors

DON E. GARNER is professor and chair of the department of accounting at the California State University, Stanislaus. He has held faculty positions at John Carroll University, Kent State University, California State University, Los Angeles, and the Illinois Institute of Technology where he was dean. He is a certified public accountant and a certified internal auditor. He is a specialist in auditing and accounting theory. His research has appeared in various professional publications including *The Accounting Review*, *The Journal of Accountancy*, *The Internal Auditor*, and *The Government Accountants Journal*.

DAVID L. MCKEE is professor of Economics at Kent State University. He is a specialist in economic development and regional economics. His research has been widely published in professional journals in the United States and abroad. His recent books include *Energy, the Environment and Public Policy: Issues for the 1990's* (edited); *Schumpeter and the Political Economy of Change*; *Hostile Takeovers: Issues in Public and Corporate Policy* (edited); *Growth, Development, and the Service Economy in the Third World*; *Canadian-American Economic Relations: Conflict and Cooperation on a Continental Scale* (edited); and *Developmental Issues in Small Island Economies* (coauthored with Clement Tisdell), all published by Praeger.